WORKING In the DARK

"I commend the authors for facing up to real-life, hard questions that people suffering with mental illnesses face in the workplace every day. The answers provided in this book are factual, practical, and easy to understand."

— *Former First Lady Rosalynn Carter*

"This wonderful book helped me come out of the closet about my depression, helped me deal with my work, and basically has been a godsend."

— *Cynthia Heimel*
Author

WORKING In the DARK

Keeping Your Job While Dealing With Depression

by Fawn Fitter and Beth Gulas

HAZELDEN®

Hazelden
Center City, Minnesota 55012-0176

1-800-328-0094
1-651-213-4590 (Fax)
www.hazelden.org

ISBN: 1-56838-790-3

Authors' note
The authors of this book are not legal or medical experts. The
advice given is based on personal or professional experience in
dealing with issues of depression and is not a substitute for legal
or medical guidance provided by professionals in these fields.

06 05 04 03 02   6 5 4 3 2 1

Cover design by Theresa Gedig
Interior design by Terri Kinne
Typesetting by Terry Webster

▪ Contents ▪

▪ Acknowledgments ▪

Beth and Fawn both wish to thank these people:
Our incomparable literary agent, Gareth Esersky, loved this idea from the beginning and worked fiercely to find it the perfect home. Every writer should be lucky enough to have an agent like her.

Three editors at Hazelden worked with us: Corrine Casanova bought the book and started the wheels turning. Todd Berger turned the manuscript into a thing of beauty and organization with dozens of small suggestions that added up to vast improvements. Karen Chernyaev shepherded it through production and into print.

To the people we interviewed, the people Beth has worked with, and our friends and acquaintances who consented to share their experiences: your stories are priceless gifts, both to us and to the readers who will see themselves in you.

Fawn's acknowledgments:
My smart, funny, fabulous co-author tops my thank-you list. Beth was ceaselessly enthusiastic in the face of tight schedules and time zone differences—and I've never laughed so hard while working on a project. Besides, all the best anecdotes are hers.

My support squad has been second to none. For writerly help, I leaned on Sarah Wernick, Niki Kapsambelis, Laura Lemay, Cynthia Heimel, Caryl Rivers, my colleagues in the National Writers Union and the American Society of Journalists and Authors, and the Byline Conference on the WELL. For sanity, solvency, and other intangible necessities, I turned to Lisa Johnson Wymer, David and Kim Daniel, Jon Katkin, Kristen Huntley, Brady Lea, Marcy Levine, David Brisson, the staff at the Blue Danube Coffee House, and—of course—my family.

Finally, my profound gratitude to Beverly Lerner, LICSW, who shone a light into the pit and helped me climb back to the surface.

Beth's acknowledgments:

The very notion of writing a book was nowhere on my radar screen until Fawn proposed we do this together. Nothing in writing can begin to express my gratitude for her bringing this "gift" to me. Our relationship as co-authors was propelled by our continuous support for each other and the fun we shared while writing this book. There couldn't possibly exist a more perfect co-author.

I have had undying support for everything I do from my husband, Ivan; daughter, Kim; and son, Jordan. Thank you for believing in me as you do. You are my world.

I am surrounded by the most wonderful friends on the planet who have listened, laughed, and given me their strength when I wavered. I would especially like to thank my mentor and lifelong friend Sally Navin, my first graduate school professor, who helped me open my mind to any possibility. I will miss her.

I'd like to thank all of my colleagues and clients who supported us in writing this book with ideas and information. Finally, I graciously thank those who confirmed the importance of writing this book with their own personal stories, as I hope this book can positively alter the lives of those who experience depression in the workplace.

· Introduction ·

Robyn was tired and irritable, struggling with work she'd once handled with ease. At first she thought she just needed a vacation. Surely she could throw off her low mood and get back to her normal, productive self if she took a few days off! But taking a break didn't improve matters. It wasn't just that she couldn't seem to get motivated; she seemed to have forgotten that she had ever been good at her job. She blew any criticism of her work out of proportion, convinced that even the mildest and most constructive feedback meant she was about to be fired. She felt frantic, desperate, tearful. She lay awake each night wondering how much longer she could keep fooling her co-workers into thinking she had any skills at all.

Then she read a list of the symptoms of depression and recognized herself in almost every one. The moment was a revelation, she says now: "I realized that I used to be happy, and I couldn't remember how that felt."

Does Robyn's experience sound familiar? If so, it's not surprising. In the United States alone, one person in twenty will have an episode of depression in any given year, and one in every five will be depressed at some point in their lives—most of them working adults who have responsibilities to meet, bills to pay, and at least part-time jobs. You could very well be one of the millions of people who take their exhaustion, hopelessness, and lack of enthusiasm to work each day. In fact, depression is so common in the workplace—thanks in no small part to overwork, layoffs, "re-engineering," and other anxiety-inducing trends—that only heart disease is higher on the list of disabling illnesses that keep people out of work.

Depression also comes with an astonishingly high price tag. A widely quoted 1993 study in the *Journal of Clinical Psychology* estimated that depression costs the United States almost $44 billion a year, including $8.3 billion in inpatient treatment, $2.9 billion in partial hospitalization and outpatient treatment, almost $2 billion in prescription medication, more than $11 billion in wages lost as a result of absenteeism, and between $6 billion and $18 billion in decreased productivity. If the study was updated to include statistics through the end of the twentieth century, one of the coauthors told us, the annual bottom line would increase to *at least $60 billion*. Imagine how that much money could be redirected if it wasn't being spent on depression!

Were any other illness so prevalent and costly, we would consider it an epidemic, declare a public health emergency, and launch preventive campaigns in every workplace. And yet even though 80 percent of people treated for depression improve significantly and lead productive lives, many employers and their health plans make little effort to combat employee depression. If you've developed depression, it's your responsibility alone to identify it early, seek treatment before it becomes too damaging, and protect yourself from its repercussions.

People with depression can feel horribly isolated in the workplace simply because depression is barely spoken about—and when it is spoken about, it's usually as a liability or weakness rather than as an illness. You may worry that if you don't seek treatment, you'll be fired, but if you do, you'll be branded for life with a big "C" for "crazy." You may suspect that if people find out about your illness, they'll think you're incompetent, unreliable, or even unemployable. As a working person with depression, you're probably preoccupied with questions like these:

- Is something at work making my depression worse or even causing it?
- Is it better to tell my boss and co-workers about my depression, or act as if nothing is wrong?
- Can I ask for time off, a flexible schedule, or other things that would make me more able to do my job?
- How much information about my illness is my employer entitled to?
- What should I do if I suspect an employer is discriminating against me?
- What can I do to "depression-proof" my daily work life?

You aren't wrestling with these things alone! Visit any support group for people with depression, sign up for a mailing list about mood disorders, or log on to a chat room discussion of the subject, and you'll soon discover how many people share your urgent concerns—and how hard it is to get accurate, useful information to resolve them.

This book is dedicated to helping you decide who and how much to tell about your illness, how to cope at work during a depressive episode, how to counter misperceptions and prejudice, and how to assert your legal rights under the Americans with Disabilities Act and other laws. We've tried to make these complex and hard-to-understand issues easier to grasp by presenting them in a question-and-answer format, with plenty of lists and summaries. In every chapter, you'll meet real people in a wide range of jobs who confronted the same questions you now face. You'll also find step-by-step guides to making your own choices based on your individual situation. We haven't so much provided answers as created a process you can follow to create answers that are right for you.

You'll get a lot out of *Working in the Dark* simply by reading it and thinking about the issues as they apply to you. We think you'll see things more clearly and make more effective decisions, though, if you keep a record of your experiences and jot down your answers to our questions. Writing things down means not having to start from scratch over and over. That's why we strongly encourage you to go through this book one chapter at a time, slowly, keeping a notebook as you read.

A note on language: Throughout most of this book, we're speaking together as "we" and "us." However, in several places, one of us speaks individually. To be clear about who's talking, we've chosen to refer to Beth in the third person (e.g., "Beth once worked with a client who . . .") but to Fawn in the first person (e.g., "When I began treatment . . .").

Writing this book has been an intensely personal experience for both of us. Beth has worked with dozens of people, in companies of all sizes, whose careers have been affected by depression. I experienced a depressive episode that left me unable to work for several months. We both have friends, colleagues, and family members who have been sidelined, discriminated against, and lost time and money to this illness. We wrote this book because we know what's at stake. The most important thing we hope you take away from *Working in the Dark* is that you don't have to remain in the dark.

▪ 1 ▪

Are You Depressed?

Depression is as common as a cold. According to the National Institute of Mental Health, it hits one in every ten Americans—almost 19 million people—in any given one-year period. If you're reading this book, you probably suspect that you're among that number. But is what you're experiencing really depression, or is it just a series of bad days? Take a moment now to consider how you've been feeling, and ask yourself these questions:

- Do you feel sad, irritable, tense, or hopeless most of the day?
- Have you lost interest in things you used to enjoy, like sex, food, or your favorite hobbies?
- Have you recently gained or lost significant weight, or noticed changes in your appetite or eating habits?
- Do you have a hard time falling asleep, snap awake in the middle of the night, or wake up early in the morning unable to go back to sleep?
- Do you feel unusually restless and unable to sit still?
- Do you feel worthless, guilty, or incompetent?
- Are you having trouble concentrating, thinking, remembering, or making decisions?

- Do you feel slowed down, clumsy, or tired all the time?
- Do you have frequent thoughts about death or suicide?

Each of these is a classic symptom of depression, but experiencing one of them now and then for a day or two doesn't mean you're clinically depressed. Everyone has an occasional sleepless night, blue morning, or cranky afternoon. If you're grieving a profound loss, like the end of a significant relationship or the death of a loved one, it's perfectly normal to mourn for several months.

Regardless of whether or not you've suffered a loss recently, if you've been experiencing either of the first two symptoms *continuously for more than two weeks*, with or without any of the others, you may indeed be having a depressive episode. If you're thinking often about harming yourself in any way, you are almost certainly depressed.

What is depression?

Everyone experiences depression a little differently. It covers a range of moods, from the low-grade chronic malaise called *dysthymia* to the wrenching anguish of a major depressive episode—yet depression is not a temporary bout of the blues. We don't yet know precisely what causes it or why some people seem to be more susceptible to it than others. One fact, though, is indisputable: although it's called a mood disorder, depression is definitely not "all in your head." In fact, it's linked to physical malfunctions in the normal processes of the brain. Explaining these malfunctions and their treatment in detail is a task far beyond the scope of this book, but this chapter will give you basic information about what depression is and what treatments are currently available.

There are actually several different categories of depression, determined by what symptoms are present, how severe they are, and how long they persist.

Major (unipolar) depression is the most widespread mood disorder, affecting 9.9 million Americans—one person in twenty—each year. Depression strikes twice as many women as men and typically begins in the mid-twenties, although people can experience their first episode at any age. Major depression falls into three subcategories:

- *Melancholic depression* typically includes feelings of slowness, lethargy, and deep sadness. In older people, it may even be mistaken for dementia. If you have melancholic depression, you probably wake at dawn, feel worst in the morning, and have little interest in eating or socializing (or anything else, for that matter). Your most characteristic emotion is apathy, and your motto is "What's the use?"

- *Atypical depression*, by contrast, includes feelings of anxiety, nervousness, and general edginess as well as hypersensitivity to other people's opinions, perceived or real. If you have atypical depression, you're probably unusually restless, but at the same time sleeping and eating more than usual, and it's likely you often feel criticized or rejected. Your slogan is "Nobody likes me." While this variety of depression is called "atypical," it's actually more common than the melancholic kind.

- *Psychotic depression*, a rare variation of major depression, includes hallucinations and delusions in addition to other depressive symptoms. Someone in the throes of psychotic depression is at a high risk for suicide and must be treated immediately.

Two other varieties of depression also share symptoms with major depression, but occur only under special circumstances. Seasonal depression, also known as Seasonal Affective Disorder or SAD, recurs every year; it's triggered by the waning sunlight of fall and lifts with the return of longer days in spring. Postpartum depression, which affects women who have recently given birth and may be linked to shifting hormone levels, can range from mild short-lasting "baby blues" to a profound psychosis that endangers the lives of both mother and child.

Dysthymia, which affects one in eighteen people at some point in their lives, is a low-level but chronic form of depression. People who are dysthymic experience mild depressive symptoms most of the day, most days, for at least two years. A study completed in early 2000 indicated that while dysthymia is "mild to moderate" compared to major depression, it becomes increasingly serious over time. In fact, about 40 percent of people with dysthymia also meet the criteria for major depression or bipolar disorder, and up to 75 percent of people diagnosed with dysthymia will experience an episode of major depression within five years.

The tragedy of dysthymia is that it often goes undiagnosed for decades. Because it often begins in young adulthood, adolescence, or even childhood, dysthymic people have been living a muted life for as long as they can remember and aren't aware that there's any other way to be. Properly treated, though, the majority recover.

Bipolar disorder, also known as manic depression, affects about 1 in 100 Americans, usually starting in early adulthood. It alternates low periods, which are indistinguishable from major depression, with periods of an extreme high mood called *mania*. During the manic phase, people with bipolar disorder feel elated, unusually creative, smarter, and more productive than ever—and in extreme cases they may act on those feelings by staying up for days at a time, spending money they don't have, indulging in risky sexual behavior, or even thinking they're invincible. Although the depressive phase of manic depression feels like a major depressive disorder, it cannot be treated with the same medications; in fact, in a person with bipolar disorder, antidepressants may trigger a manic episode.

* * *

While no one has determined yet what causes depression, studies of brain function offer certain clues to where it may begin. In recent years, research into antidepressant medication has shed some light on the way the brain works and what happens when something goes wrong. The brain secretes neurotransmitters—chemicals such as serotonin, norepinephrine, and dopamine—which speed electronic impulses between nerve cells, enabling the brain to tell the body what to do. The newest antidepressants seem to work by increasing the level of neurotransmitters in the brain, suggesting that a chemical imbalance may be the root cause of depressive symptoms.

Because people sometimes slide into depression after an injury, illness, loss, or other traumatic event, it's also possible that external happenings affect the chemical soup in the brain. However, scientific studies are inconclusive about whether trauma *causes* depression or whether some people are simply closer to depression in the first place and therefore more likely to "tip over" into it in times of distress. While no one has pinpointed specific depression genes yet, years of research throw substantial evidence behind the idea of biological predisposition: people whose parents, siblings, or other close relatives have experienced depression are at higher risk than the general population. If you have such a family history, you should be especially aware of the symptoms of a depressive episode in order to recognize and treat it as soon as possible.

What are my medical treatment options?

Your general practitioner may be willing and able to write you a prescription for antidepressants, but it would be better to make an appointment with either a psychiatrist (a medical doctor who specializes in mental health) or a psychopharmacologist (a psychiatrist who further specializes in medications for mental illnesses and mood disorders). These doctors have in-depth knowledge of mood disorders and the most up-to-date information about antidepressants, and their specialized expertise is the best route to the most appropriate treatment and the proper follow-up care over time. A psychiatrist will consider the length and severity of your symptoms, any other medications you may be taking or that you may have taken in the past for depression or any other illness, and your overall health history before deciding which of the currently available medications is most likely to work well for you.

By now, it seems like everyone knows someone who's taken Prozac, which was touted as a "wonder drug" when it came out and became a household name seemingly overnight. Today, Prozac is probably second only to Viagra in name recognition. But there are actually almost two dozen frequently prescribed antidepressants, as well as new ones in development. The following chart gives an overview of some of the medications your doctor may suggest, including their most common trade names (some medications are sold under several names).

Medications for Depression

Medication Class	Generic Name	Trade Name	Possible Side Effects
SSRI (selective serotonin reuptake inhibitor)	citalopram hydrobromide fluvoxamine paroxetine fluoxetine sertraline	Celexa® Luvox® Paxil® Prozac® Zoloft®	Nausea Insomnia Sleepiness Agitation Sexual dysfunction
Aminoketone	bupropion	Wellbutrin®	Agitation Insomnia Anxiety
SSNRI (selective serotonin norepinephrine reuptake inhibitor)	venlafaxine	Effexor®	Agitation Nausea Dizziness Sleepiness Sexual dysfunction
SSRIB (selective serotonin reuptake inhibitor and blocker)	trazodone nefazodone	Desyrel® Serzone®	Nausea Dizziness Sleepiness
Tetracyclic	mirtazapine	Remeron®	Sleepiness Weight gain Dizziness
Tricyclic	clomipramine amitriptyline desipramine nortriptyline doxepin trimipramine imipramine protriptyline	Anafranil® Elavil® Norpramin® Pamelor® Sinequan® Surmontil® Tofranil® Vivactil®	Sleepiness Nervousness Dizziness Dry mouth Constipation High overdose toxicity
MAOI (monoamine oxidase inhibitor)	phenelzine tranylcypromine	Nardil® Parnate®	Potentially fatal interaction with all above Dizziness Dangerous interaction with some foods
SNRI (selective norepinephrine reuptake inhibitor)	reboxetine	Vestra®	Dry mouth Constipation Increased sweating Insomnia
SRA (seratonin reuptake accelerator)	tianeptine	Stablon®	Dry mouth Anorexia Nausea Flatulence Gastralgia

Your doctor is most likely to start your treatment with one of the SSRIs, which have proven to be equally effective as the older tricyclics and MAOIs with fewer side effects. However, everyone's brain is different, and an antidepressant that works wonderfully for one person may have no effect on another.

As with any prescription drug, always follow your doctor's advice on how and when to take your medication. Also, use the many resources available online and elsewhere to learn as much as you can about potential drug interactions. You may learn that some substances you thought were harmless have unpleasant effects when combined with a particular medication. For example, dextromethorphan—a cough suppressant commonly found in over-the-counter cough syrups and cold remedies—can cause hallucinations when taken with Prozac (and possibly other SSRIs).

Taking an MAOI requires particular vigilance, as certain foods interact with this class of medication to cause hypertensive crisis, a sudden and potentially fatal increase in blood pressure. If you're taking an MAOI, plums, raisins, and bananas are forbidden fruit—as are cured meats like sausage and salami, caffeinated drinks of all kinds, most kinds of cheese, chocolate, avocados, spinach, yogurt, tomatoes, and several other common foods. Fortunately, the newer generation of antidepressants are prescribed far more often than MAOIs, so you probably won't need to restrict your diet for the sake of your mental health.

Do *not*, under any circumstances, adjust the dosage or mix medications without your doctor's advice. As we've already mentioned, coming up with the right dosage can be a delicate balancing act, and a medical professional's expertise is necessary to ensure you're taking neither too much nor too little for the best results with the fewest side effects. More important, some medications are dangerous when taken together. In particular, combining an MAOI with some other antidepressants can result in hypertensive crisis, stroke, and possibly death. If you're changing from one medication to another, your doctor may require you to taper off the first medication and allow it to leave your body entirely before starting the second. Follow your doctor's instructions to the letter.

Is St. John's wort a safe herbal alternative to medication?

First, let us emphasize that if you're using, or intending to use, St. John's wort, it's crucial that you let your doctor know. St. John's wort should not be taken at the same time as a prescription antidepressant. If you're taking prescription medication and want to try St. John's wort, or vice versa, you must allow several weeks for whatever you're taking to leave your system.

As for the herb's effectiveness, the evidence is mixed. In early 2001, the *Journal of the American Medical Association* published a study suggesting that in cases of chronic major depression, St. John's wort is no better than a placebo. A year earlier, however, German researchers concluded that for mild to moderate depression, St. John's wort works just as well as the tricyclic antidepressant imipramine (Tofranil), with fewer side effects. Clearly, more research is needed.

In Germany and some other European countries, St. John's wort is licensed and widely studied, with labeling and use controlled and standardized. However, in the United States, herbal medicine is barely regulated at all. So the good news is that St. John's wort is readily available without a prescription in the United States—but the bad news is that it comes in many forms, from loose herbs and teas to tinctures and capsules, and there's no easy way to determine the standard dosage. How many tea bags, in how much water, steeped for how long? Is the herb fresh, or is it getting old and stale? How many capsules should you take? The lack of standardized labeling and dosage makes it hard to tell what you're getting, or even whether every dose contains the same amount of the herb. Also, unlike prescription drugs, it's up to you to determine how much to take and how often. Do your research, buy only reputable brands, and talk to a professional herbalist if possible. Above all, pay attention to your physical reactions. Although it's "natural," St. John's wort is still a medicinal plant and should be used with care and respect. If it makes you feel worse rather than better, stop taking it immediately.

Will taking an antidepressant jeopardize my recovery from chemical dependency?

Some people in recovery are hesitant to take antidepressants. They believe taking medication means they aren't working their program properly, or they fear that antidepressants are mood-altering substances that will lure them back into addiction. Both of these concerns are understandable, but unfounded. We firmly believe that proper treatment for depression can only bring you closer to sobriety and serenity.

Neither Alcoholics Anonymous nor other Twelve Step programs forbid antidepressants. Indeed, an AA pamphlet called *The AA Member—Medications and Other Drugs* reassures readers that "just as it is wrong to enable or support any alcoholic to become readdicted to any drug, it's equally wrong to deprive any alcoholic of medication which can alleviate or control other disabling physical and/or emotional problems." Moreover, antidepressants are not addictive. Unlike mood-altering drugs with fast-acting results, antidepressants take several weeks to achieve any effect at all. When they do, they cause not euphoria or numbness, but a sense of stability.

That being said, if you're recovering from chemical dependency, you may have particular medical concerns that need to be addressed if you plan to take antidepressants. For example, you may need to talk to your doctor about how the medication will affect a damaged liver, or whether you'll be able to take your prescription in the proper way at the proper time every day.

You'll find a detailed discussion of depression and recovery in Patricia L. Owen's beautifully written and easily understandable book, *I Can See Tomorrow: A Guide for Living with Depression*. You may also wish to read *The Dual Disorders Recovery Book*, a guide to the Twelve Steps for people with both addiction and mental illness. Both are available from Hazelden.

Should I see a therapist?

In 1989, the National Institute of Mental Health (NIMH) conducted an extensive study comparing the effectiveness of psychotherapy and antidepressant medication in treating major depression. The conclusion: medication alone was far more effective than therapy alone. However, subsequent research—and common sense— indicate that the best possible treatment is not one or the other, but both.

Medication is the fastest route out of the black pit where everything is hopeless and nothing seems possible. But after the medication has taken hold, you need to learn (or re-learn) how to live a depression-free life without the familiar bad habits and negative thought patterns you've developed. That's where therapy comes in. A good therapist will also teach you how to recognize the onset of another episode in order to cut it short.

The NIMH called interpersonal therapy, or IPT, one of the most promising types of psychotherapy. Originally developed specifically for people with major depression, ITP is an intensive short-term (twelve to sixteen weeks) process that focuses on improving relationships with the important people currently in the patient's life by teaching the patient new adaptive skills.

The other psychotherapy used on depression with great success is cognitive-behavioral therapy. This form of therapy, also short-term, teaches patients to notice how they tend to leap to the most negative conclusions and gives them an arsenal of behavioral strategies (like relaxation techniques) and cognitive techniques (like generating positive rather than negative conclusions) to replace their pessimistic thought processes.

What about electroconvulsive therapy (ECT)?

For a tiny minority of people with depression, the only treatment that works is electroconvulsive therapy, or ECT. Although many people associate ECT with Jack Nicholson's character in *One Flew Over the Cuckoo's Nest*, who was shocked into mindless submission, modern ECT is quite different. It's given under anesthesia and a muscle relaxant; the patient feels no pain and awakens after a few minutes.

ECT is used in only three circumstances: in cases of depression so severe that the patient is likely to harm himself without immediate relief; in situations where the patient can't physically tolerate medication; and in cases of "treatment-resistant" depression where no medication has been adequate. In general, ECT's side effects are mild—post-treatment headaches and sleepiness—but some people experience memory problems.

What are my prospects for recovery?

With treatment, your chances of making a full recovery are excellent. Our knowledge of mood disorders and the human brain have advanced so rapidly in recent years that more than 80 percent of people who pursue treatment for depression improve significantly in just a few months. This is true whether they're being treated for their first episode or long-term depression. Like other serious illnesses, depression gets worse if it's left untreated, even if, in your depressed state, you can't tell that you're feeling worse. Early diagnosis and treatment can make all the difference; research shows that depressive episodes become more severe and more frequent over time.

Of course, you can always choose not to be treated. NIMH studies show that most people recover from a depressive episode within six to twelve months even without treatment. But with treatment, recovery time drops to two to four months and recurrence drops off dramatically—while 10 to 15 percent of all people with untreated depression eventually commit suicide. Don't suffer unnecessarily—or risk your life!—when help is readily available and highly effective. However long you've been battling depression, any time is a good time to seek a cure.

How long will my treatment last?

This is a question best taken up with your doctor and therapist. At the very least, you should continue for several months after your depression lifts. Work closely with your doctor to determine the best medication for you at the dose you can best tolerate with the most positive results. You may be fortunate enough to find the right combination of medication and dosage right away, or you may need to spend a few months tweaking the two until they work. Keep in mind that it takes up to a month to see any significant improvement, and at least two months for maximum effect. In the next chapter, we'll discuss what depression looks like at work, and we'll offer suggestions on how to cope there until the positive effects of treatment begin.

· 2 ·

Not Just Another Bad Day
at the Office

Joanne has walked away from three consecutive jobs—one because the workload felt overwhelming, one because she felt trapped between two squabbling colleagues, and the third because it required a long, tedious commute. Each time, she simply went home one day, never to return, then spent the next few weeks dodging calls from baffled bosses and concerned co-workers who wondered where she was and whether she was all right. One former employer has no idea, to this day, why Joanne never came back to work.

"When I'm uncomfortable, I feel paralyzed," she explains. "I don't feel like I can do anything about it. It's easier just to leave, even though I feel guilty about it afterward." As a result, Joanne's career seems to be stuck in reverse—every job she takes requires less work and less responsibility than the one before.

Maybe you feel overwhelmed, stressed out, and frustrated. You know you're letting people down, and you don't know what to do about it. Maybe you're furious that they expect so much more than you think you can handle. Or maybe you just can't drum up the energy to make an effort. As you read through the next section, think about your behavior and feelings at work. Do you suspect depression is behind your problems?

What does depression look like at work?

Depression manifests itself in a wide range of feelings and behaviors. We've listed some of the ones you're most likely to experience, beginning with the most common.

- *Problems concentrating.* Almost everyone having a depressive episode experiences this symptom. It shows up in several forms: impaired short-term recall (forgetting things you've just done), gaps in long-term memory (forgetting policies or procedures that used to be second nature), or an all-encompassing inability to process information. Carina, for example, found herself reading memos as if they were written in a foreign language, going over them slowly a dozen times before they made sense. Eventually, she gave up and simply sat at her desk, surrounding herself with paperwork that made her look busy.

- *Loss of energy.* The exhaustion and insomnia typical of depression can overwhelm even the most energetic people. Linda was one of those people, ordinarily spending long hours at her desk, but depression left her feeling like a run-down battery in desperate need of a jump start. By lunchtime, she was struggling to stay awake.

- *Feeling slowed down or feeling restless and unable to sit still.* Some depressed people describe themselves as "being stuck in slow motion" or "having a lead blanket draped over my brain." Their physical reactions slow with their mental agility—a potentially life-threatening hazard. What happens if the driver of an 18-wheeler doesn't hit the brakes soon enough? What if a construction worker's power tool slips? What if a police officer fumbles with a gun?

Others say they feel jittery, easily distracted, "like a hamster is running on a wheel in my head." They may be unable to settle down to one particular thought, or even sit still, for more than a few minutes.

- *Irritability.* When everything seems directed at you personally, it's difficult to control your temper. Nicole became hyper-defensive whenever she thought she was being criticized, sullenly disagreeing with her co-workers and even her boss. She also lashed out at clients when they called to check on late deliveries, snapping, "What do you mean, you didn't get them?" She was eventually asked to resign.

  Among men, in particular, depression often shows up as outright anger. Whenever anyone disagreed with Raoul, he took it as a personal attack. A tall, imposing man, he banged his hand on the table and shouted, his face red with rage, until he intimidated his "opponents" into backing down. When his employer began to worry he would attack someone physically, Raoul was placed on probation with two choices: get help or resign.

- *Feeling worthless, guilty, or anxious.* Whenever Robyn's boss called her into his office, she felt nauseous with fear. Even the mildest criticism convinced her she was about to be fired, and she suspected any praise was intended merely to butter her up and prevent her from looking for another job until the company could hire her replacement. Even though no one had ever complained about the quality of her work, she was certain she had no talent, no promise, and no chance of landing another position if she lost this one.

- *Apathy.* At the other extreme, pessimism can flip over into indifference. If you feel nothing you do makes any difference, it's easy to stop putting any effort into your responsibilities. Gary, for example, was ordinarily a stickler for detail in his reports. He researched them meticulously, wrote them painstakingly, edited them to perfection, and even specified the font he wanted used in the final copy. But during his low times, his reports were carelessly researched, obviously padded with material leading to irrelevant conclusions, and rife with misspelled words and misplaced punctuation.

■ *Problems making decisions.* You may find yourself unable to make even the smallest choices: Answer the phone or let it ring? Buy black pens or blue ones? Get a turkey sandwich or a garden salad for lunch? Larger or more complex decisions may be paralyzing. Michaela, an attorney, asked for advice on cases that should have been simple matters. After she caused repeated delays and errors handling an important client's routine business, the directors of her firm decided not to promote her to partner.

■ *Isolation.* Nessa deliberately took on assignments that required her to work alone, either behind her closed office door or in the library. Once she stopped going to lunch and participating in office life, it was easy for others to label her "not a team player." Trying to hide depression by avoiding co-workers can backfire badly; although her performance is still satisfactory, the perception that she's an unreliable loner may force Nessa to find another job where she won't have to carry the baggage of her reputation.

■ *Avoidance.* Joanne, whom you met at the start of this chapter, began to ignore her duties as bookkeeper at a nursing home, choosing instead to spend most of the day talking to friends in online chat rooms. After being warned that she would lose her job if her performance didn't improve, she called in sick every morning for the next week—almost as if she was *asking* to be fired rather than taking responsibility for wanting to leave.

How can I get through the day until I start feeling better?

You may decide to use sick time or take a brief leave of absence rather than try to work in the worst of the crisis, but although your depression is undoubtedly cutting into your concentration and productivity, you may not be so incapacitated that you can't function. More importantly, you probably don't have the luxury of unlimited time off. You'll need to plan ways to cope—to set your depression aside for a few hours a day—until treatment takes effect and your mood starts to lift.

A depressive episode is like any other serious illness: you have to take care of yourself so you'll have the strength to cope. Would you push yourself to achieve if you were undergoing chemotherapy? Treat yourself with generosity and patience.

- *Avoid major changes in your daily routine.* Dramatic change causes stress, and stress will only make you feel more overwhelmed and out of control. This is no time to switch to the night shift, transfer to another city, or volunteer for overtime.

- *Cut back on your responsibilities and hours wherever possible.* Don't do it on your own, of course; get your supervisor's cooperation and approval. You may think that if you aren't around, no one will notice that anything is wrong, but your absence may actually draw attention to the changes in your behavior. Don't make the same mistake Guy did when he decided to set his own hours, either working shortened days or coming in at lunchtime and staying late into the night. Since no one could be sure he'd be around when he was needed, he became a convenient scapegoat whenever anything went wrong. In fact, he nearly lost his job because it was so easy for other people to blame mistakes on him. After all, he wasn't there to defend himself.

■ *Make a point of putting in "face time."* When you're depressed, isolation is tremendously tempting. Many depressed people have trouble organizing their thoughts, feel numb or raw, or are convinced they have nothing of value to say to anyone. But the more you isolate yourself, the easier it becomes to convince yourself that you're a liability—and the less visible you are, the more you jeopardize your job. Go out of your way to spend time with your co-workers. Look for ways to work in a group; this will give your work and work relationships structure and purpose. At the very least, have lunch with your workmates as often as possible. Interaction will remind you that you have something to contribute, and you'll stay "in the loop" at a time when your natural inclination is to hide out. Above all, don't succumb to the temptation to use up your sick time on days that you just don't feel like showing up. You may need time off for other medical reasons later.

■ *Ask questions rather than trying to carry a conversation.* Whether you're at lunch or in a meeting, you can't just sit there while everyone else talks. It doesn't look professional, and it only amplifies your feelings of anxiety and worthlessness. When you can't manage to participate fully in the conversation, ask questions. If you just can't think of what to ask on the spur of the moment, write out a few questions beforehand and refer to your notes. Your questions will keep other people talking while still allowing you to be, and look, involved.

- *Pay attention to your appearance.* Neglecting your appearance—or even your cleanliness—will only make you look as bad as you feel. At the same time, you aren't just putting a good face on your bad day when you put on a freshly pressed uniform or a flattering, appropriate outfit. If you dress to impress, then behave as if you feel every bit as capable and qualified as you look, you may act yourself right into a productive day. A receptionist at a busy front desk explained it this way: "My job requires a lot of person-to-person contact, and I need to act upbeat no matter how lousy I feel, so when I'm at work, I think of myself as a character in a play. Putting on the smile and the behavior can be really hard, but focusing on the part I'm playing takes my focus off the depression and puts it on what I'm supposed to be doing."

  Psychologists know that changing the way you act is an effective first step toward changing the way you feel. Twelve Step programs have an evocative name for this behavioral trick: "acting as if." Try it—it works!

- *Make time for yourself in your schedule.* When you're filling in your appointment book, make time for a mental health break every day. Some days, you may want to schedule an hour at lunch to see your therapist or visit a support group. Other days, you may just have five or ten minutes to spare; on those days, try venting behind closed doors to a close work friend or reading from a daily meditation book kept in your desk drawer. If you decorate your workspace with personal items (photographs, office toys, postcards) that remind you of good times, you can glance up for a shot of optimism any time.

■ *Plug in to online support.* If you have Internet access at work, you have an unparalleled resource at your fingertips. Use a search engine on the World Wide Web to find basic information about diagnosis and treatment, learn about medication and therapy, and check up on current research. Then visit one of the many support groups online to ask for advice and share personal experiences with other people who understand how you feel. Of course, you shouldn't devote your working hours to browsing the Internet, but a few minutes of research during your lunch break may inspire or reassure you just enough to get you through the afternoon. We've provided a few recommendations in the appendix to get you started.

However, be aware that, by law, employers are allowed to monitor your online use to ensure you aren't spending too much work time on personal pursuits. If you're using a workplace Internet account to visit depression-related sites, to subscribe to a mailing list about mood disorders, or even to order a medication refill from your local pharmacy, be aware that someone, somewhere, might have a record. If you think you have good reason to be concerned about confidentiality, either find out the company policy *before* you start surfing, or save it until you get home.

■ *Conserve your energy.* Schedule your most important work for early in the day, before you use up what little reserves you have. If you can find a place where you won't be disturbed, try taking a catnap during your lunch break; you may find as little as fifteen or twenty minutes of snoozing refreshes you. Unless your doctor has recommended cutting out caffeine, allow yourself a cup of coffee when you need it. If you're struggling with insomnia, talk to your doctor about what you can do to improve your sleep habits and ensure you get the rest you need.

- *Seek privacy at difficult times.* A crying jag might make you feel better, but it can disconcert your co-workers. If you find yourself bursting into tears unexpectedly, find a private place, like the rest room or a vacant office, either to let it out or to get it under control so you can return to your work area composed. You may decide at some point to reveal to your colleagues that you're struggling with depression (we'll discuss how to make that decision later in this book), but until then, it's best not to give them the impression that you can't handle yourself professionally.

- *Fit exercise into your day.* Take a vigorous walk at lunch, go to an exercise class at the end of the day, commute on your bike—just do something to move your body and get your circulation going. When you work out, your body produces endorphins, chemicals that cause feelings of pleasure and well-being. What better reason to head for the gym?

  You may even discover that exercise releases your pent-up feelings of anger or despair and gives you a new sense of direction. When Gina fought her lethargy by enrolling in an aerobics class, she came to love it so much that she's now working toward certification as a fitness trainer.

- *Eat well.* In today's hectic, gotta-do-it-yesterday work-place, it's easy to slide into a diet of microwave burritos and lukewarm soda. Eating poorly can wreak havoc on anyone's waistline and overall health; some evidence even indicates that what you eat can affect your mood directly. In fact, a few years ago, a popular book suggested that fighting depression was a matter of trading Prozac for potatoes! The truth is, you probably can't eliminate your depression entirely by changing your eating habits, but eating right never hurt anyone—and modifying your diet may well help you feel better. Your doctor may be able to suggest ways to adjust your eating habits, or you may want to work with a nutritionist. If you experience noticeable changes in your mood when you eat or don't eat certain foods, you may also want to ask your doctor to test you for food allergies.

We know it's hard to resist the quick, easy temptations of the drive-through and the vending machine, but try bringing your meals from home or, at the very least, choose the healthiest meals from the options available to you in the company cafeteria. And while we're on the topic of what you consume...

■ *Avoid alcohol.* Alcohol is a depressant. Why work against the relief you crave? Also, if you're taking antidepressants, you'll probably find that anything more than a minimal amount of alcohol gives you a throbbing headache or intoxicates you more quickly than it ordinarily would. Over time, you may learn you can have a small drink from time to time without suffering any ill effects, but particularly at the beginning of your treatment, there's no point tossing fuel onto the depressive fire.

■ *Ask for changes in your work situation as needed.* Consider asking your employer for part-time hours, a telecommuting arrangement, a schedule change, or some other practical adjustment to help you stay productive. Present it not as something you need to make your job easier, but as a tool to increase your effectiveness. As we'll discuss in the next two chapters, this is called "reasonable accommodation" and, if your depression meets certain criteria, you have a legal right to it under the Americans with Disabilities Act. Of course, if you are requesting significant change in your job structure, you will likely need to make a decision about revealing your depression to your employer, a choice examined in detail in chapter 5.

If I take medication, will it affect my work?

You're probably wondering how taking antidepressants will influence your ability to get things done. You'll most likely have to cope with side effects as you work with your doctor to find an appropriate treatment. Ironically, although most antidepressants take three to six weeks to have a positive effect on your mood, their side effects tend to start after just a few days. Many people are fortunate enough not to experience any side effects, but it's possible you'll find yourself distracted by insomnia, dizziness, headache, dry mouth, drowsiness, stomach upset, or some other reaction you weren't expecting.

Many people who take antidepressants report that at first they feel energized and even a little jittery, as if they'd had a bit too much coffee. But some people react in the opposite way. I spent my own first two weeks on medication feeling as if someone had slipped me a dose of knockout drops. Although I got out of bed every morning at my accustomed time, I felt as though I was still asleep. I yawned constantly. I drank cup after cup of coffee simply to stay awake. By late afternoon, I was so drowsy that I was terrified to drive for fear I'd doze off at the wheel. And by evening, normally my most productive hours, I found myself falling asleep on the couch—and, once, at my desk with my head on the keyboard.

I finally complained to my doctor that being sleepy all the time was adding to my misery and erasing what little ability to work I still had. She cut my dosage of medication in half and recommended I take it at bedtime instead of first thing in the morning. Presto—the sensation of being sedated disappeared quite literally overnight. The change enabled me to stick with treatment so that, one morning not long after, I woke up and realized the depression had begun to dissipate as well.

The most unpleasant side effects do tend to wear off over time, usually within a few months. If they're extreme, however, or if they don't fade away, speak to your doctor. Medication is supposed to make you feel better; if it's making you feel worse, it's not doing its job.

***

Just as depression shows up in various ways, coping with it requires varied strategies. Explore any option you think might help—and keep a record so you can remember what works. If your depression tends to recur, having a plan in advance will help you ride out the next downturn. Discuss with your doctor what time of day to take your medication. Be willing to adjust the amount and type of medication you take, if necessary. Track your low-energy times so you can try to schedule around them. Take care of yourself physically and emotionally. Most importantly, while you search for a treatment that provides some relief, remind yourself that the period of adjustment is well worth tolerating for a little while in order to be depression-free.

· 3 ·

Is My Job Driving Me Crazy?

In 2000, when the United Nations' International Labour Organization (ILO) surveyed office workers in the United States, Germany, the United Kingdom, Finland, and Poland, it reached a shocking conclusion: at any given time, up to 20 percent of office workers suffer from depression, anxiety, or a related mental health problem. That's *one person in five* working in an office. The ILO pointedly blamed this high percentage on work itself: unpleasant or dangerous conditions, dysfunctional corporate politics, a hypercompetitive global economy that keeps the deadlines coming with no downtime, and new technology that makes it ever easier to blur the line between work and leisure.

Why is the workplace turning into a breeding ground for mental illness? What's behind this high rate of malaise? We believe that in many ways, it's because our society has decided to put the bottom line first. If profits come before people, it's easy to shut down departments or entire companies with no advance notice and no severance pay. It's easy to see employees as interchangeable, disposable parts who can bear the blame for problems and be replaced on a moment's notice. And it's easy for people caught up in the turbulence to blame themselves for not keeping up with the market. Besides, when it comes to running a business, taking individuals' needs and skills into account is much more complicated than balancing the books. Put it all together, and you can see how easy it is for people to end up being the last ingredient to be valued in the organizational recipe.

Even though depression is often biological in origin, there's no question the stress of an unhealthy workplace exacerbates it. In fact, researchers from Johns Hopkins University's School of Public Health have gone so far as to say work stress *causes* depression. "Not having much say at work and having a high workload increases the occurrence of a condition known as job strain," study coauthor Dr. William W. Eaton said in an interview with *Reuters Health*. "Somebody with high job strain is five times more likely to have a depressive disorder compared to someone with low job strain." It's worthwhile to give some serious thought to whether your job is making your depression worse—or even whether it's the main factor.

How do I determine whether my job is the problem?

Ask yourself this:

Am I right for this job? Is this job right for me?

In order to find the answers, you'll have to examine yourself and your work closely by asking yourself a series of other questions. We've come up with an exercise to help you through the process.

First, get a notebook and a pen so you can *write down* your thoughts. This is important! Answering these questions in your head may help you realize that something is wrong, but the best way to explore the issues fully is to write down your answers—seeing things in your own handwriting has a remarkable way of clarifying vague ideas and uncovering trouble areas. Next, schedule a quiet time for the exercise, when you know you won't be disturbed for at least half an hour. Once you begin, spend about five minutes on each of these questions:

- Does my work keep me stimulated, challenged, and interested? If not, do I feel like I could do it with my eyes shut? Or, conversely, do I feel like I'm overwhelmed by more than I can handle?

- What are my strengths? Does my job take advantage of them, or does it force me to ignore or even work against them?

- What do I enjoy doing? Am I doing something I like to do, or am I doing something I hate but happen to be good at?

- Am I gaining experience with every year, or am I having the same year of experiences over and over? When was the last time I learned something?

- Are my surroundings physically comfortable? If not, why not? What kind of discomfort or pain am I experiencing?

- Is the atmosphere emotionally comfortable? If not, why not? How do I feel when I get ready for work, while I'm at work, when I head home?

- Where can this job take me—and is it someplace I want to go? If I stay on this career track, if I get the next logical promotion, if I stay at this company— will I end up doing something other than what I'm good at and want to do?

You may want to spread this exercise over several days in order to give your focused attention to one question at a time. The deeper you go into each one, the more accurately you'll be able to pinpoint the source of your discomfort.

Do I have a problem boss?

Joachim's boss was famous for getting good work out of her employees, and notorious for the way she accomplished it: by browbeating them into compliance. Rather than telling people how to improve their work, she chose to "motivate" her employees by telling them they were lazy and talentless. Her compliments were rare and always followed by a torrent of personal abuse.

"Anyone with self-esteem quickly moved on, so the office was full of 'lifers' who had stuck around to vie for the approval of this person who was never going to give it," Joachim recalls. "One woman had been there for ten years and had never gotten a raise because she was terrified to ask for it."

At the time, Joachim didn't think he was depressed; he just thought he hated his boss. In retrospect, though, the signs were clear. Most mornings, he could barely drag himself out of bed to go to work, and when he got there, he felt angry, frustrated, and resentful most of the time. He finally decided that being unemployed with no new job in sight would be better than working for someone who managed by intimidation. He quit and soon found a better-paying job elsewhere. Interestingly enough, he later learned that at least two of his former co-workers had taken medical leaves due to depression, and several others were seeing therapists who eventually advised them to quit.

Of course, it's rare for a boss to be so thoroughly lacking in management skills that she literally drives employees crazy. But your immediate supervisor has a profound influence on your day-to-day work life, and a toxic boss creates a toxic environment. Does your boss set unrealistic deadlines? Make excessive demands? Harass you verbally? Abuse you physically? Don't let your feelings of powerlessness turn into depression. Be angry about the way you're being mistreated, not about your inability to make it stop.

Beth once worked with a company where one of the top managers had an obvious problem with his temper. One day, he lost control completely: in the middle of a screaming rant, he picked up a bookcase and threw it at his assistant. Needless to say, the manager was suspended. As for the assistant, she didn't blame herself, and she didn't stick around to see what would happen when he came back. Wise decision. Don't hang around hoping your problem boss will turn into a decent human being. When someone is dumping garbage on you, saying "stop that!" is much less effective than simply getting out of the way.

Are my co-workers making me nuts?

Does work bear a disturbing resemblance to being back in junior high, complete with cliques, gossip, bullying, and all the unspoken rules that determined who was "in" and who was "out"? No wonder you're feeling uneasy. If you're stuck in a company where internal alliances and coalitions take precedence over getting the work done, you're practically guaranteed to be uncomfortable. When you have to battle interdepartmental squabbling, your frustration grows. When your ideas are rejected, ignored, or even belittled, how can you not question yourself?

At a certain weekly magazine, for reasons no one could quite pinpoint, two departments had developed such a fierce rivalry that employees from those departments avoided each other in the cafeteria and deliberately dragged their heels on deadlines, even though they had to work closely to create the finished product. Half the employees spent more time fighting or anticipating a fight than actually working. Meanwhile, those trying to stay out of the conflict were tugged back and forth by co-workers trying to get them to take sides by dragging out years-old grudges and perceived snubs. The constant tension and sniping reduced several normally mild-mannered staffers to snarling cranks as they tried to work without being either attacked or ostracized.

Am I being asked to do too much with too little?

Just ask any teacher in a cash-strapped school district what it feels like to handle a full classroom of children with books that were out of date 15 years ago and not enough pencils to go around. If you're being asked to do too much with too few resources, you may take it as a challenge at first, but after awhile, you're almost inevitably going to feel stuck.

This is a common problem in companies that have gone through heavy layoffs and expect the remaining employees to pick up all their departed co-workers' slack. The layoff "survivors" end up working twelve-hour days to do themselves what used to be spread out among many more people. When you're facing insufficient time, money, equipment, or other people to share the load, your first and most frequent thought will probably be, "There's no way I can keep up." After awhile, you'll probably find yourself adding, "…so why try?"

Are my skills or education going to waste?

Surprisingly, not having enough to do can be just as stressful as being overextended. Gita was excited about her prospects when she accepted a post at a corporate library, but it didn't take long for her to realize that rather than helping employees find information, she was spending most of her days salvaging books they'd spilled coffee on and throwing away trash they'd left behind. "Of course I'm not satisfied at work," she says. "I'm not a librarian; I'm a maid."

It's frustrating and stifling to suspect that you could be making so much more of a contribution if only you were allowed to. Maybe you're working at a job far below your talents and abilities. Maybe you're in a position where you have to jump through so many hoops to get permission to act that you've given up on ever getting anything done. Either situation can lead to frustration and a lack of motivation to produce, which in turn can lead to depression.

Is it hard to figure out what I'm supposed to be doing?

Does your employer keep changing the company rules, policies, procedures, or strategy with little notice and less explanation? Whether you're stocking shelves at the supermarket or plotting takeovers in the boardroom, it's hard to feel like you fit in at your job when you're getting mixed messages (or none at all) about your duties and goals. It's as though you're expected to decipher a secret message with no codebook.

Some employers make this mistake from day one, throwing new hires into their new positions with little support. No one tells them who's who, where to find information and supplies, or how to get up to speed on the tasks they've just inherited. Sometimes they aren't even told where the bathroom is! With no idea how to navigate the company's culture, people reach out to whoever's nearest and seemingly helpful—and just as in high school, where slipping into the "wrong crowd" earned you a bad reputation until graduation, making the wrong alliances at the office can be career suicide.

When the rules are up for interpretation, the person with the most power gets to be the interpreter. That leads to turf-building, back-stabbing, and other power grabs as everyone struggles to be in charge, and before you know it work starts to feel strangely like an episode of *Survivor*. Of course, some people thrive on the challenge of keeping up with chaos, but most of us find it upsetting and anxiety-producing. There's nothing wrong with wanting consistency and clear guidelines from one day to the next.

Am I getting feedback that doesn't make sense?

Does your employer say your performance isn't up to snuff, but leave you wondering what you can do differently? If you think you're doing a great job, of course you're going to be disappointed if someone says otherwise. But a negative or lackluster review isn't useful without specifics about what you can do better. The point of feedback—be it a written report or simply a comment made in passing—is to give people a chance to improve by setting benchmarks they need to meet. Otherwise, it's too vague to be useful.

If someone says you need to improve your communication skills, where do you begin? You deserve to know not just what you need to change, but how you'll be able to tell that you're doing better, and how much time you have to reach your goals. Without these measurements, you're never done; you're always on the hook, never quite sure that you're getting where you need to go. Incomplete, uninformative feedback puts you in a position of having to read minds in order to deliver what people want. Unless you're a professional psychic, that's a no-win situation.

Am I running as fast as I can and getting nowhere?

Do you feel overwhelmed and out of control with no prospect of relief? Does your employer require you to carry a beeper around the clock and respond to pages at any hour of the day or night? Do you have so many deadlines that you take work home on weekends and haven't been able to use your vacation time in years? Are you working two jobs because neither one alone pays you enough to make ends meet? Whatever the cause, if you're constantly racing to keep up with all the demands on your time with no end in sight and no way to ask for a break, something has to give.

Leigh Ann was a registered nurse on a medical/surgical floor of a large hospital, caring for five or six extremely sick people simultaneously on any given day. One patient might need an IV, another a pitcher of water, a third to be helped to the toilet, while everyone's families were looking to her for reassurance and information. She awoke at 2 A.M., worked a twelve-hour shift with just one half-hour break, and had few nonwork activities because being on duty different days each week made planning regular events almost impossible. Over time, Leigh Ann developed severe insomnia; when she did manage to sleep, she had nightmares. She became irritable, snappish, tearful. One of her co-workers eventually told her she didn't seem like herself and suggested she talk to someone at the hospital's Employee Assistance Program (EAP).

"All the EAP did was refer me to an outside counselor," she says. "And while my supervisor did decrease my workload by giving me less critically ill patients, that only lasted a short while, and my request to work the same days every week was turned down. I was told that if I got that, everyone would want it."

Leigh Ann has concluded that while she might be prone to major depression, the real source of her problems has been the high drama, fast pace, and erratic schedule inherent in hospital nursing. "It's not just me, it's the way the job is structured," she insists. After staying home for several months to get her depression under control, she's decided that rather than going back to the hospital, she's going to look for work in a doctor's office or as a nurse consultant for an insurance company—positions that include all the aspects of nursing she loves but with regular hours and much less stress.

Is my job just a bad match overall?

Bill's first bout with depression happened just a few years into his career as a computer programmer. Worried about money after a layoff, he took the first offer to come along, even though it involved a type of programming he didn't enjoy or understand very well. "I started getting into a cycle of sitting and staring at my screen without working, or obsessing over irrelevant details," he says. "I stayed at the office later and later, caught up in small, meaningless tasks I felt compelled to finish before I could move on to what I really needed to do. Then I'd be so tired in the morning that I'd go in late, or call in sick. I got so far behind that I couldn't catch up and couldn't bear the thought of trying."

He quit, but with no savings, he panicked and leaped at the first available job. Once again, it was a job he didn't like, and the cycle of procrastination and avoidance continued. Bill's next step was to move to another city, where he found a job he genuinely enjoyed: programming for an arts organization. The work was exciting and stimulating, but the pay was low, so he left for a lucrative but dull position as a computer jockey in a financial services firm. "I knew it was a bad decision at the time, but I needed the money, so it didn't seem like I had any options," he reflects. "And then the cycle started again. I didn't finish assignments, I came in late, I kept saying I was working when I wasn't, I was making excuses for why things weren't getting done. One day my manager took me out to lunch to discuss strategies for improving my performance, and then two weeks later he called me in and fired me."

Adding up the evidence, Bill reached an important realization: working just for the sake of a paycheck is hazardous to his mental health. Back in the market again, he's making it clear to recruiters that this time he's only interested in working for certain companies, in certain industries—even if it means he has to take a pay cut to do it. "The only other option is to keep taking jobs I hate, not doing the work, and getting fired."

I think my job might be the problem, but what can I do about it?

Problems come from conflict, which looms especially large for people with depression. You may see problems as being your own fault, completely out of your control, or even both at once. You may be tempted to quit rather than try to figure out what the problem is or how to fix it. But after reading this chapter, you probably have some ideas about what's going on and whether there's anything you can do to make things better. Which of these four categories of conflict does your situation fall into?

1. People are operating on different data and don't know it. If you've been told you have until tomorrow to complete a task, but your co-worker thinks it needs to be done in the next hour, of course you're going to butt heads! Your co-worker will think you're dragging your heels, you'll feel pressured, and neither of you will understand why the other isn't cooperating. You can solve this conflict by figuring out where the misunderstanding lies and finding a way to make sure that everyone is reading from the same page, so to speak.

2. People can't agree on the "right" way to reach a goal. A

chef and a waiter both have the same goal—to serve diners a fresh, hot, tasty meal—but perhaps the chef believes it's best to send food to the table as soon as it's ready to be served, while the waiter thinks it's better to wait until everyone's meal is prepared so everyone can be served at the same time. This kind of conflict requires people either to find procedures they can both agree on or to agree that the way the work gets done is less important than getting it done well.

3. People have different goals. The manager of a coffee shop that ordinarily closes at 7 P.M. wants to stay open until midnight so he can offer an alternative social scene to people who don't want to go to bars. His employees, all students, don't want to work that late on school nights. Again, communication is the solution to this conflict. The manager could extend the café's hours on Friday and Saturday nights only, or offer a bonus to employees willing to stay late on weeknights. The employees could agree to work until 9 or 10 P.M. By compromising, no one wins, but no one loses, either.

4. People have different core values. If the conflict in values is huge, your choice is simple: knuckle under and sacrifice your values, or cut your losses and leave. When Tranh asked for time off to help his mother recover from surgery, his boss asked why he couldn't just send his wife. That response made it clear to Tranh that he was expected to put work first even in a family crisis—an expectation that violated all his beliefs about being a loving son and husband and a caring human being, and which he couldn't possibly meet. But in less extreme cases, there's usually a middle ground. For example, imagine a company with two teams that have to work together. One has a more flexible manager who permits

flextime and telecommuting and is relaxed about the process of meeting goals. The other manager is more autocratic and commanding, with a high value on "face time," procedures, and timelines. These two managers have to work together, and they each feel that finding a way to do that forces them to compromise their values: in her case, work/life balance, and in his case, putting the company first. However, as long as her team agrees to be available when needed, and his team is less rigid about its timeline, the compromise isn't unbearable for either.

If you find your job intolerable, you need to make some decisions about how to handle the situation. Doing nothing will only fuel your feelings of helplessness, which in turn will amplify your depression. You may choose to confront the problem directly by telling your employer about your discomfort and pushing for change, or you may decide you're better off simply putting a bad situation behind you.

If you like what you do, but not where you're doing it, you may merely need to find a similar position in a more functional company. But if you've realized that for whatever reason there's a broader mismatch between you and the work you're doing, it's time to start considering other options. Regardless of the appropriateness of the position, if you're in an actively dysfunctional situation, do all you can to get out—even if it means temporarily taking a pay cut to do it. No salary is worth your mental health.

What kinds of resources are available to help me?

We're enthusiastic advocates of career counseling as a tool as you explore what's available to you in the working world. A good career counselor can help you with many aspects of your work life, such as clarifying your vocational skills and interests, finding resources to help you explore new opportunities, and supporting you in your job search.

A career counselor can also administer the Myers-Briggs Type Inventory, or MBTI, an instrument to help you determine what situations are easier and less stressful for your particular personality. We consider the MBTI a uniquely useful tool for people with depression. Through a series of questions about your preferences in various hypothetical situations, the MBTI determines how much you're energized or drained by interacting with other people; how much you make decisions based on intuition or hard facts; whether you're inclined more to the emotional or the logical; and how strongly you prefer closure to the open-ended. Once you're aware of your natural tendencies, you'll have valuable information about how you might be at odds with yourself. For example, if you're a strong introvert, someone who needs a lot of time alone to recharge, working in a sales job that requires you to talk to strangers all day long is likely to exhaust you. Once you know what your preferences are, you can find jobs and environments that are more aligned with them.

Additional professional advice at very little expense is as close as your neighborhood bookstore or public library. Here you'll find dozens of books to help you determine what jobs and companies are a good fit with your skills and personality, investigate new opportunities, and create possibilities you haven't considered before. The appendix includes a list of books we particularly like.

Your local adult education program is another low-cost resource. Check out catalogs from university extension programs, nonprofit and private continuing education organizations, and community centers. You'll find dozens of classes that run the gamut from learning new software to starting your own business, all at prices that won't overextend your wallet.

If you went to college, take advantage of your school's career center. Many schools offer their alumni career counseling and placement for nothing (or next to nothing). Some even have extensive resource libraries.

In addition, many state unemployment departments offer services like skills assessment, vocational training, help with your job search, and information about the local labor market. In some cases, you may be eligible for intensive one-on-one career counseling and case management at no cost.

Finally, the Internet offers dozens, even hundreds, of sites devoted to career development and job hunting. Check out the big job boards like Monster.com, plug the phrase "career counseling" into your favorite search engine, and sign up for a few mailing lists in industries or fields that interest you. You'll be astonished at all the information you turn up.

* * *

It's one thing to be unhappy at work. It's another thing entirely to discover that you've missed out on a raise, a promotion, or an opportunity because someone thinks you're too depressed to do your job. Fortunately, laws passed to make the American workplace more hospitable to people with physical disabilities may also protect you. We discuss those laws and their ramifications for you in the next three chapters.

· 4 ·

The Americans with Disabilities Act and You

It may seem like a huge and overwhelming task to assert your rights when you're also struggling to overcome depression, but you can begin by knowing what your rights are. In the United States, several laws say you're entitled to fair treatment in the workplace—that employers cannot discriminate against you just because you suffer from severe depression. The most far-reaching and important of these laws is the Americans with Disabilities Act, or the ADA.

What is the Americans with Disabilities Act?

The ADA protects people with mental and physical disabilities from discrimination in employment, public transportation, state and local government services, public accommodations, and telecommunications. The law applies to companies with fifteen or more employees (including part-time employees). It doesn't apply to Native American tribes, the U.S. government, or tax-exempt private membership clubs. Parts of the ADA do not apply to religious organizations.

The ADA is often referred to as "the Civil Rights Act for the disabled." This is no exaggeration. Since the day it was signed into law (on July 26, 1990), the ADA has been every bit as significant in protecting the rights of the disabled as the Civil Rights Act is in protecting the rights of minorities.

What do the various sections of the ADA cover?

The ADA has five sections, or titles, dealing with various aspects of discrimination. We'll be talking about three of them in particular: Title I, Title II, and Title III.

Title I of the ADA requires covered employers to provide equal opportunity to qualified individuals who happen to be disabled. It forbids them to ask about health conditions, including mental health, before making a job offer. It also requires them not to discriminate against the disabled in job application procedures, hiring, advancement, firing, compensation, and training, among other things. This section is probably the one most relevant to your concerns as a person with depression.

Title II prohibits discrimination by state and local government agencies. This section of the law covers all public agencies whether or not they receive federal assistance, and it guarantees access to all programs, services, and activities provided by a public agency, including public education, employment, recreation, health care, social services, courts, voting, and town meetings. Under Title II, you may not be turned away from a publicly funded job, class, event, or service just because of your depression.

Title III prohibits discrimination by private entities and nonprofit service providers operating public accommodations. This includes privately operated entities that offer licenses and exams, private schools and colleges, banks, restaurants, theaters, hotels, private transportation, supermarkets, shopping malls, museums, health clubs and other recreational facilities, sports arenas, doctor's offices, lawyer's offices, and insurance offices, and other commercial facilities. These public accommodations must not exclude people with disabilities, segregate them, or treat them unequally. Although this section of the ADA is best known for requiring curb cuts, wheelchair ramps, and other amenities that make buildings more accessible to people with physical disabilities, it also requires employers to make reasonable modifications to their policies, practices, and procedures. Just as important, it requires employers either to offer licensing and certification classes and exams in places and ways that are accessible to people with disabilities, or to provide alternative accessible arrangements. For people with depression, this may mean being able to take exams while hospitalized or being allowed additional time to complete coursework necessary for a license.

Titles IV and V of the ADA address issues that aren't directly relevant to your concerns as someone with depression. Title IV deals with making telephones and television programs accessible to people with hearing and speech disabilities. Title V talks about enforcement issues, such as how the ADA relates to other laws and how agencies can develop materials to help businesses comply with the law's requirements. Title V also specifies certain behaviors that are excluded from coverage by the ADA, including compulsive gambling, kleptomania (compulsive stealing), pyromania (obsession with setting fires), cross-dressing and other sexual behaviors, and disorders caused by current illegal drug use.

Why is the ADA so important?

Congress passed the ADA for two reasons: first, to fight discrimination against people with disabilities, and second, to counterbalance the myths, fears, and stereotypes that discrimination is based on. In fact, one of the standards for determining whether you're eligible for protection under the law is whether other people consider you unable to perform a job, *even though you're perfectly capable and qualified*. Quite simply, if you encounter bias in the workplace because of your depression, the ADA is your first line of defense.

I'm not in a wheelchair, I can see and hear, I have all my limbs—does the ADA apply to me?

That depends on one thing: how severe your depression is. It's true that many people who ask for the law's protection are disabled by ailments ranging from blindness to back problems, but the ADA embraces any condition, *physical or mental*, that causes problems severe enough to make daily life markedly more difficult than the average person's.

The Equal Employment Opportunity Commission (EEOC), which enforces Titles I and III of the ADA, has received so many questions about how the ADA protects people with mental illness that it's issued detailed reports, called "enforcement guidances," which address a wide variety of related legal issues. The EEOC received 2,858 complaints in 1999 alone from people with a mental illness who suspected their employers were discriminating against them. Of those complaints, almost half involved depression.

You may be extremely uncomfortable with the notion of calling yourself "disabled." You may even feel, as one woman told us, that your depression, however serious, seems trivial next to an obvious physical disability, or that calling depression a disability somehow insults people who can't see or are missing a limb. That's perfectly understandable! None of us likes to feel that we've been reduced to a label, and many of us feel embarrassed or even ashamed to admit having problems we can't handle on our own. However, if you can show that your depression impairs your daily life enough to be considered a disability, the ADA protects you, too.

How do I know if my depression is serious enough to be a disability?

The ADA is extremely specific about what "disability" means. In order to meet the law's definition of disability and qualify for its protection, you *must* be able to show that your depression fits into one of these three categories.

1. *It substantially limits your ability to perform major life activities.*

   In addition to obvious things like breathing, seeing, and hearing, "major life activities" include learning, thinking, concentrating, caring for yourself, interacting with others, speaking, performing manual tasks, sleeping, and working. If you have dysthymia or mild to moderate depression, you're probably able to do all these things fairly well and make it from one day to the next in spite of your symptoms. If you've been struggling with severe depression, though, it may be causing substantial limitations. Limitations are substantial if performing major life activities is *significantly* more difficult for you than it is for the average person.

   Here's an example: Say you've been depressed for several months. You've been unable to sleep more than a few hours a night, you rarely leave the house except to go to work, you find yourself thinking obsessively about your problems, and you often feel weak and ill because you have no desire to eat. Your impairment, major depression, is significantly restricting your ability to sleep, interact with others, concentrate, and care for yourself, and it has been doing so for some time. Therefore, your depression is disabling.

2. *It has substantially limited you in the past, even if it isn't doing so now.*

   If you can prove that at some point in your history, you were unable to perform a major life activity because of your depression, you're covered by the ADA. Let's go back to the previous example: after several months of substantially limiting depression, you see a psychiatrist who starts you on a successful course of treatment. Even though the depression lifts and you regain your ability to do the things you once struggled with, the law continues to protect you from discrimination.

   This definition of disability also applies if your depression is cyclical—that is, if episodes of disabling depression alternate with times when you're able to function well, whether or not you're being treated. Since you go through periods of being substantially limited, you can still be considered disabled even during the times that you're feeling better.

3. *Other people perceive you as being substantially limited by your condition, even though you actually aren't.*

   This definition of disability may be particularly important to you, especially if your depression isn't substantially limiting. Let's be blunt: Depression still carries enough of a stigma that you may find yourself battling not just your illness itself, but other people's misguided notions that a depressed person is crazy, weak, or simply unable to do a good job. You might be seen as lazy, incompetent, or potentially dangerous *regardless of your actual abilities*. You may even be accused of making the whole thing up as an excuse to avoid responsibility. Despite the law, it is possible an employer will discriminate against you because you've admitted to having bouts of depression, or because you were once hospitalized for depression many years ago. We don't like it any more than you do, but it happens. Fortunately, that kind of prejudice qualifies you for the protection of the ADA even if there's no evidence that your depression is disabling or has interfered with your performance in any way.

What do I have to do to claim my rights under the ADA?

The first thing you have to do is tell your employer that you have a disability. (Yes, the law essentially asks you to acknowledge and document your limitations at the same time you're trying to prove you're qualified to work—an awkward position to be in.) But you don't have to say you're depressed. You can be extremely vague—saying, for example, that you have "an illness" or "a biochemical imbalance." We'll discuss exactly what to say and whom to tell in the next chapter; we'll even provide you with a script to follow if you need it.

Because depression is more or less invisible, in a way that more obvious physical problems aren't, you probably won't be able just to say "I'm disabled." Your employer will most likely ask you to verify your claim. You can do this by presenting evidence that shows how depression is substantially limiting your ability to perform major life activities at work, at home, and elsewhere. In addition to your own spoken or written words, you can also ask your family members, friends, or co-workers to describe, verbally or in writing, how it affects you. You must also prove that it has lasted for more than several months (or, if you have recurring depression, that it's likely to come back) and that it has significantly restricted your ability to perform at least one major life activity during that time.

You may choose to present documentation from a doctor,

psychiatrist, or therapist who is familiar with your condition. Of course, doctors and other health care professionals often assess their patients' health for work-related purposes, but they're also bound by professional requirements to respect your confidentiality. If you're asking your own doctor or therapist to document your health, be aware that your employer is only entitled to information about whether or not you're fit to work—*not* the details of your diagnosis and treatment. If you have to be examined by a doctor when you're hired, the doctor should tell you clearly what information will be passed along to your employer.

So if my depression is disabling, what *am* I entitled to under the ADA?

If your depression meets the law's criteria for disability, employers must treat you the same as any other qualified employee. They also have to give you certain kinds of help you may need to be able to perform your job well. This help is called "reasonable accommodation."

What is a "reasonable accommodation"?

A job accommodation is a change or adjustment to a job that makes it possible for an otherwise qualified person to perform the duties necessary to the job. Accommodations are "reasonable" when an employer can provide them without "undue hardship," that is, without an excessive financial burden or excessive interference in the way the business operates. Under the ADA, an employer *must* make accommodations as long as they aren't unreasonable. Obviously, your employer's finances and operations will determine whether a particular accommodation is reasonable—a large, well-funded company is capable of much more than a small business with only a few employees. By and large, though, the kinds of accommodations useful to someone with depression are more likely to be minor adjustments than huge projects.

Because having a depressive episode is invisible compared to lacking an arm or being unable to hear, employers sometimes have a hard time understanding how someone struggling with depression could possibly be disabled, and an even more difficult time understanding what kinds of accommodations might be helpful. In a May 19, 1997, article about workplace discrimination against people with psychiatric disabilities, *Time* magazine noted that many managers have been quicker to install expensive wheelchair ramps than to accommodate their employees who might need flextime or the occasional day off for treatment—this even though "accommodating the mentally ill...often requires little more than an attitude adjustment."

It just makes good business sense for companies to make sure all their employees can do their jobs as well as possible. More importantly, reasonable accommodations are not special privileges; they're your civil rights.

How do I know what kind of accommodations to request?

Go through the following process step by step to determine what kinds of accommodations will be helpful to you.

First, figure out what the job's essential functions are—that is, the basic requirements of the position. These are the things you absolutely must do as part of the job. The EEOC defines a task as "essential" if it meets one of these criteria:

- The job exists to perform the function.
- A limited number of employees at the company are available to perform the function.

- It's a specialized task, and people are hired specifically because they have the expertise or ability to do it.

If you're still in the interview process, ask for a detailed job description. Pay close attention to all the requirements so you can anticipate what your day-to-day responsibilities would be. What will you need to be able to do to meet those demands? If you're already at work, ask for a copy of your written job description, if you don't have one, and go through the same process. What do you absolutely have to do in order to meet your responsibilities? What tasks are important, but not central to the job?

Next, consider how your depression might interfere in any way with your ability to perform those essential functions. Do you have problems remembering things? Concentrating? Managing your time? Controlling your emotions? You may want to refer back to chapter 2 as you think about how depression affects you at work. Remember that side effects from your medication, such as drowsiness or dry mouth, may also qualify as functional limitations if they're severe enough. Think about the ways in which you can get around these limitations.

Now think about your work environment. Does anything about it increase your stress, distract you, or make your work more difficult? Look back at chapter 3 for suggestions on thinking this through.

Finally, put it all together by making three lists.

1. What strategies or accommodations would improve your ability to perform the job's essential functions? If you're not sure, keep reading—we've provided a list of accommodations other people have found useful.

2. What would make your workplace less stressful or dis-

tracting? Again, the list of potential accommodations can point the way.

3. What can you change, what do you need your employer's help to change, and what will you just have to find a way to live with?

These questions don't have one-size-fits-all answers. Some people have trouble concentrating in busy offices, while others find that being surrounded by noise and bustle actually helps them focus. Some people are intensely upset when their work has to go through other people before approval, taking it as an insult to their competence. Other people are comforted to know they have the safety net of another person's attention to ensure they haven't made any mistakes. For every person who wants a flextime arrangement, someone else will prefer to work the same hours as everyone else. The accommodations that work for you will be unique to your own needs. You may even decide you don't need them at all.

What are some common accommodations?

The Job Accommodation Network (JAN), a federal agency that offers free advice on employing people with disabilities, has successfully helped people use accommodations like these:

- Exchanging nonessential duties with co-workers so that you can focus on your primary responsibilities.

- Arranging for your job description to change very little over time, to ensure your job doesn't shift to include duties you're unable to perform.

- Using "to do" lists to ensure you know what needs to be done and can keep track of whether you've done it.

- Using a computer or electronic organizer.

- Receiving instructions in writing as a way to improve your recall of important details.

- Meeting regularly with a supervisor to discuss workplace issues and performance.

- Working with a job coach (a vocational rehabilitation expert who helps people develop skills and tactics to help them overcome the limitations of a disability) to help you manage assignments, set priorities, meet deadlines, or interpret feedback.

- Taking short but frequent breaks to improve concentration.

- Wearing headphones and listening to soft music to screen out distracting sounds while you work and to improve your ability to concentrate.

- Having high cubicle walls installed, or moving into an office with a door that closes, to minimize distractions from passing co-workers.

- Moving your desk to a quieter location with less foot traffic.

- Working part-time.

- Working a flexible schedule ("flextime")—for example, working 7 A.M. to 3 P.M. or noon to 8 P.M. instead of 9 A.M. to 5 P.M., or working four ten-hour days instead of five eight-hour days.

- Job-sharing.

- Working from home all or part of the time.

- Taking time off for medical or therapy appointments and making up the lost time later in the day or week.

- Using vacation or personal time for medical time off if you've already used up your sick leave.

- Taking an unpaid leave of absence.

These are just a few examples; you and your employer should come up with solutions that fit your particular needs. If you're having a hard time coming up with options, or if you find the whole process confusing, you may want to turn to a counselor or job coach for advice. You can also ask for help from JAN or the ADA Disability and Business Technical Assistance Centers. You'll find more information about these organizations in the appendix.

As you think about your own needs and your own workplace, you may discover that the tactics and solutions that would work best for you don't require you to involve your employer at all, or can be done without mentioning your depression or asserting your legal rights. Or, if you realize the most useful changes you can think of are related to your depression, you can ask your employer to make them as accommodations under the ADA.

What other laws protect me against discrimination at work?

The Family and Medical Leave Act of 1993 (FMLA) may give you certain rights in the workplace. The FMLA, which is enforced by the U.S. Department of Labor, allows certain employees to take up to twelve weeks of unpaid leave each year without losing their jobs or health benefits. The FMLA applies to local, state, and federal government agencies and local schools as well as companies that employed fifty or more employees in twenty or more work weeks in the current or preceding calendar year and are engaged in commerce or in any industry or activity affecting commerce—including joint employers and successors of covered employers.

In order to be eligible for leave under the FMLA, your depression needs to be considered a "serious illness." This is a much less rigorous standard than the ADA's requirement that you be disabled. The FMLA defines "serious illness" as an illness, injury, impairment, or physical or mental condition that is incapacitating—that is, which makes you unable to work or perform other daily activities—and that requires either inpatient treatment or ongoing care. You must give your employer a thirty-day notice of your intention to take time off, if possible; you may also have to provide documentation of your illness, get a second or third opinion (at your employer's expense), or update your employer regularly of your status and intention to return to work.

Your employer must continue to pay your health benefits while you're on FMLA leave, although it can demand reimbursement if you don't return to work after your leave is over, and with certain specific exceptions, you must be allowed to return to your job or an equivalent job on your return.

I work for the U.S. government, which is exempt from the ADA. What laws protect me?

If you work for the federal government, the law that applies to you is Title V of the Rehabilitation Act of 1973, the first legislation to prohibit discrimination against people with disabilities. The Rehabilitation Act, which uses the same standards as the ADA to determine employment discrimination, applies to federal agencies and programs conducted by federal agencies.

The Rehabilitation Act also applies to businesses with federal contracts as well as organizations and programs that receive federal funds, such as colleges participating in federal student loan programs. These businesses, organizations, and programs may also fall under the ADA.

I work in state government, and I heard that the Supreme Court decided the ADA doesn't apply to state employees. Is this true?

Not exactly. The Supreme Court ruled in February 2001 that state employees may not sue in federal court for monetary damages under Title I of the ADA, the section of the law that mandates equal opportunity for the disabled in the workplace. This does not mean state employees are no longer covered by the ADA! This case (*University of Alabama* v. *Garrett*) was an extremely specific ruling focusing on whether Congress can force states to pay money damages under federal law. It does not affect any other provisions of the ADA. State employees with disabilities can still turn to the ADA, as well as state law, administrative procedures, and the U.S. Equal Employment Opportunity Commission, for protection against discrimination.

Am I still protected by the ADA if my treatment is working well?

As of this writing, the only honest answer we can give you is "maybe."

In the American legal system, laws are enforced based not just on the legislation as written, but on courtroom decisions that interpret the law. Every time a court decides a law should be applied in a certain way, every subsequent case has to take that decision into account. The ADA says that any substantially limiting impairment is considered a disability, whether or not there's some way to correct it (called a "mitigating measure"). However, in 1999, the Supreme Court decided in two separate cases that if an impairment can be corrected to the point where the person has little or no problem performing major life activities, it doesn't meet the first definition of "disability."

In the first case, *Murphy* v. *United Parcel Service, Inc.*, the delivery company argued it was justified in refusing a man a delivery job because his high blood pressure made him a danger to himself or others behind the wheel. The plaintiff said his illness was a disability that didn't prevent him from performing the job in question, and that therefore he was a victim of discrimination. The Court ruled that the plaintiff was not disabled because he could lower his blood pressure by taking medication, and that therefore UPS's refusal to hire him was not a violation of the ADA.

In the second case, *Sutton et al.* v. *United Airlines, Inc.*, an airline turned down two women who applied to be pilots because they were both extremely nearsighted without corrective lenses. The plaintiffs argued that since they could use contact lenses or glasses to meet the job's specific vision requirements, the airline was being discriminatory in refusing them jobs they were otherwise qualified for. The Supreme Court ruled that since the women could wear glasses to correct their vision, their myopia didn't qualify as a disability, and that therefore they weren't protected by the ADA.

The *Murphy* and *Sutton* decisions say that an impairment is only a disability if it can't be corrected. At the same time, confusingly, they suggest that employers can reject applicants for having impairments even though, once corrected, the impairments don't stand in the way of the applicant's ability to do the job. While *Murphy* and *Sutton* dealt with plaintiffs who had physical impairments, the decisions have disturbing implications for people with psychiatric disabilities: People whose depression is disabling because it isn't fully controlled by treatment need the ADA less, simply because they're less likely to be able to perform the essential functions of a job in the first place. Meanwhile, those whose depression is under control are more likely to be in the workplace, and therefore more likely to encounter discrimination, but will have a much more difficult time defending their rights.

In other words, you can only invoke the ADA as protection against workplace discrimination if you can prove you're disabled. But if you've found treatment that eases your depression enough that it no longer causes serious problems in your day-to-day life, you may have a difficult time proving that you meet the law's definition of "disability."

So if I'm taking antidepressants, that means I have no legal protection against discrimination?

That's not entirely accurate. For one thing, the ADA is a federal law, and even if it doesn't apply to you, state law might. State supreme courts are not required to follow the U.S. high court's lead. As we were writing this book, two states—New York and California—had already chosen not to apply the Supreme Court's interpretation of the ADA to their states' antidiscrimination laws, and a third, Massachusetts, was considering the issue. You'll want to investigate your state's laws as this question comes to more and more courtrooms on the state level.

As for the situation at the federal level, the Supreme Court has made proving disability more difficult—but not necessarily impossible. The Judge David L. Bazelon Center for Mental Health Law, a nonprofit organization in Washington, D.C., issued a report in 2000 on the implications of the Supreme Court's 1999 decisions. The report noted: "The mere fact that an individual takes medication or other mitigating measures . . . does not mean that he is not a person with a disability. Determining whether someone has a disability now requires a very careful analysis of what limitations the person continues to experience *despite medication and/or therapy*" (emphasis ours).

If treatment hasn't fully controlled your depression, or

if your depression returns from time to time in spite of treatment, you can argue that the ADA still covers you. Likewise, if the side effects of your medication are severe enough that they qualify as substantial limitations themselves, that's an argument in your favor. And the ADA continues to protect you if you can prove you suffered from disabling depression in the past, even if you're fine now.

Finally, the ADA continues to protect you against the *perception* of substantial limitation, that is, if people assume your depression limits you more than it truly does. Just be aware that if you take action against an employer on this basis, you'll have to demonstrate that the discrimination was based on someone else's fears and stereotypes. Although it's not easy to prove how other people see you, we'll be talking more in chapter 6 about steps you can take to improve your chances of doing just that.

If I can prove the ADA applies to me, do I have an edge in the workplace?

In a word, no. If you have the same qualifications and necessary skills as other applicants for a position, and reasonable accommodations will make it possible for you to do the job, an employer is not allowed to turn you down simply because you're disabled. On the other hand, an employer is not required to hire, promote, or keep you simply because you have a disability. You must have the skills to perform a job's essential functions—the main duties of the position—with or without reasonable accommodations. In other words, you can't *have* the job if you can't *do* the job.

Here's a basic example using an obvious disability: A talented graphic designer with management experience who happens not to have legs can't be refused the job of art director at an ad agency simply because she needs a desk she can comfortably use from a wheelchair, although she can be turned down in favor of a more qualified applicant.

The law requires employers to be flexible about how work gets done, as long as it gets done properly and well. The law does not require employers to change the qualifications for a job or lower their performance standards. Returning to our person in a wheelchair, what if she applied for a job at a moving company? She could probably drive a moving van retrofitted with hand controls, but an essential part of working as a mover is the ability to lift furniture and climb in and out of the back of the truck. Since no accommodation would enable her to carry out those duties, the moving company would be within its rights to refuse her the job.

But aren't accommodations special privileges? I'm afraid I'll look greedy.

You may sometimes hear the argument that accommodating someone with a disability is giving that person preferential treatment over other employees. The truth is, most employees, disabled or not, need help from time to time so they can perform at their best. For example, someone caring for a sick child may need to work from home for a few days. Someone working in a poorly lit office may need a bright desk lamp. The kinds of accommodations that will help you succeed at work in spite of your depression will probably be equally small and inexpensive. Many accommodations—allowing you to work a flexible schedule, for example—cost nothing at all. As a matter of fact, JAN reports that for every dollar a company invests in accommodating an employee who is disabled, it actually *gets back* an average $34.50 in increased productivity and decreased expenses. JAN offers advice to more than 40,000 people a year, and on average, its recommendations cost less than $500 and return more than $5,000 in benefits to the employers who implement them.

When should I ask for accommodations?

When you realize you need them. That might be before or during a job interview, after the interview but before you've received an offer, after you've received the offer but before your start date, during your first day, or at any time after that. Martine, for example, had been at her job for two years when she began taking medication to treat her depression and asked for a long lunch break once a week so she could visit her doctor.

There's also no limit to either the number of times you're allowed to ask for accommodations or how often you're allowed to ask. You may request one reasonable accommodation during your first week on the job and another three months later. You may take advantage of a reasonable accommodation for a period of time, decide you no longer need it, and then request it again at a later date. Since accommodations are about what you personally need to do your job well, the timing depends on your individual situation and needs, and no one else's.

How do I ask for accommodations, and who do I talk to?

As we've already mentioned, in order to receive accommodations under the ADA, you must tell your employer that you have a disability and spell out how it limits your ability to function. You must also ask for the specific accommodation you want and explain how it will help.

You don't have to go into detail about your diagnosis, symptoms, and treatment, but you do have to disclose enough information to support your request. We realize that you probably feel incredibly uncomfortable disclosing *anything* about your depression, and we acknowledge there are good reasons for being anxious about it. You may be worried that saying anything at all will only make things more difficult. In the next chapter, we'll walk you through the process and help you decide how to have the conversation and who to talk to. We'll also explore situations in which it makes more sense not to mention your depression at all.

· 5 ·

To Tell or Not to Tell

Telling your employer about your depression, and determining how much to say, is a major decision, and not one to be made lightly. Considering how many people still have inaccurate and prejudicial misconceptions about mood disorders, even hinting about your illness can make finding and keeping a job more difficult than it needs to be. Your best protection against discrimination may be simply to say nothing. If you've found treatment that controls your depression enough that it doesn't interfere substantially with your life, you probably have no reason to mention it. You aren't required to tell anyone that you take medication, see a therapist, or participate in a support group, any more than someone who once had a broken leg needs to discuss it once the cast comes off and the crutches go into storage. As long as you're meeting all your goals and responsibilities at work, your diagnosis is no one's business but your own.

On the other hand, if you're feeling good and doing well, there's probably no better time to mention that you have a potentially disabling illness that your boss and co-workers may someday need to accommodate. If you're making a formal request for job accommodations, you must explain to the person responsible for arranging the accommodations what you need and why you need it.

Otherwise, you're under no obligation to say anything at all to anyone. You may decide, however, that being open about your condition is simply easier than trying to keep it a secret. What's more, you may find, to your surprise and satisfaction, that your boss and colleagues are much more supportive than you dreamed they would be.

Sarah repeatedly warned her supervisor that working in an understaffed office while mothering a young child was stretching her beyond her limits. As a result, when she slipped into a depressive episode, explaining the situation was just the logical next thing to do in a process she'd started months earlier. She asked for several weeks off to reduce her stress level and improve the chances of successful treatment. Her employer granted her a paid leave and, when she returned, allowed her to switch to a four-day work week with hours starting at 10 A.M. In addition, Sarah successfully argued that she would be more efficient and effective if she were allowed to hire an assistant.

"They've been tremendously understanding and accommodating," she says. "I don't feel I've lost any ground professionally as a result of this."

Few employers will be as remarkably responsive, but most employers will at least try to meet your most pressing needs. However, they can't meet your needs if you don't speak up about having them.

What do I need to think about to make this decision?

These are the questions you'll need to answer for yourself as you determine what and how much to tell:

- Which will be less stressful: to disclose my depression or to guard my privacy?
- Who am I thinking of telling? My immediate super-

visor? My contact in human resources? My team-mates on a specific project? Everyone in my depart-ment? Everyone in the office?

- How much do they already know about my depres-sion or depression in general? Do they seem to be well-informed, or at least open-minded?

- Why am I thinking of disclosing? Am I asking for accommodations? Do I think making people aware of my depression will improve my work situation? Do I want them to understand something about depression?

- How much do they need to know, given my reasons for wanting to tell?

- What questions and concerns might they have, and how will I address them?

Why might I want to disclose?

- You need a job accommodation. In this case, you must disclose, since the ADA only requires employ-ers to accommodate disabilities they know about.

- You think making your co-workers or supervisor aware of your depression will make it easier for you to work together.

- You've decided that hiding your depression takes too much effort. You'd be happier and more produc-tive if you could direct your time and energy toward something else.

- You work in a place where people aren't just co-workers, but friends. You and your colleagues talk about personal issues as well as professional ones, you support each other through difficult times, and you know they care about you and will be there for you if you need them. Bianca revealed to two friends at work that she was nearly immobilized by depression. In a remarkable act of generosity, they offered to take on all but the most essential aspects of her job so that she could focus on recovery. They screened her voice mail, e-mail, and inbox to weed out anything that didn't require her direct input, returned phone calls for her, and even helped her prepare for meetings she couldn't avoid. The benevolent cover-up went on for several months; to this day, no one else at their workplace suspects that their friendship saved Bianca's job.

- You want to demonstrate by example that depression doesn't have to be a liability in the workplace. You've decided that by doing your job well and talking openly about your depression, you can improve other people's work situations as well as your own. You may be considering "turning lemons into lemonade" by sharing your experiences and knowledge with your co-workers through informal conversations, or even by volunteering to lead educational workshops.

Why might I want to keep my depression to myself?

- You don't feel it interferes in any significant way with your performance and therefore doesn't need to be mentioned. For example, many people with mild to moderate depression are able to function perfectly well on the job; their work gives them something to focus on.

- You simply aren't sure what to say about it. You don't have the time, energy, or interest to invest in explanations, so it's easier to say nothing.

- You're afraid your co-workers will think you're getting special treatment and you don't want their resentment to get in the way of working as a team.

- You'd prefer to keep your personal issues—health and otherwise—out of the office. For example, Justin was an intensely private person who shrank from any kind of public display, from birthday cards to a note of appreciation in the employee newsletter. The idea of disclosing his depression was unthinkable.

- You're concerned that people will judge you and your work based on their stereotypes about depression rather than your actual skills and abilities. Sandy, who describes her position as "somewhere between management and clerical," says she's certain no one at work would ever take her seriously again if they knew. "I've heard co-workers joke about being nuts or using mental illness as an excuse for not doing real work," she says. "The last thing I want to do is give them any reason to question my competency."

- You're worried that your employer will use your illness as an excuse to fire you, pass you over for a promotion, refuse you a raise, or discriminate against you in some other way, regardless of the law.

How do I get ready to disclose?

Your first step should be to prepare yourself by gathering all the information you need about yourself, your depression, and your workplace. This process may take you several weeks.

1. First, arrange support ahead of time so it's available to

you both as you prepare and when you disclose. If you're working with a job coach, let him or her know you're planning to disclose, and ask the coach to be present at the meeting. Devote some of your therapy time to talking about this issue; your therapist can rehearse your disclosure with you and even help you draw up a script you can follow. You may even want to invest in a single meeting with an attorney who specializes in employment law to be sure you understand your rights and responsibilities as well as your employer's.

2. Observe your employer's approach to diversity in general, and mental illness in particular. The more obvious it is that your company values people based on their skills and abilities, the more likely it is that you're working in a supportive and open-minded workplace. Do you see newsletters, notices on bulletin boards, and other evidence that your workplace is open to many different kinds of people? Does your employer offer training classes, mentoring, telecommuting, flextime, and other programs designed to help employees contribute at their highest level? Are benefits packages tailored to individuals rather than one-size-fits-all? As far as you can tell, has the company hired anyone else with a disability, and has it been a positive experience for the company and the employee? If you have health insurance through your employer, does it cover both mental and physical health?

3. Keeping your observations in mind, and referring back to chapter 3 if you need to, ask yourself where your workplace falls on the spectrum between healthy and dysfunctional. Is it a safe place to be different or vulnerable? Does management say one thing ("we promote diversity") but do another (the range of acceptable

behavior is narrow, and no one who "sticks out" gets promoted)? Does your human resources department have a reputation for being supportive and upholding confidentiality? Pay attention to what you see and hear. If people become visibly uncomfortable around anyone who's "different," you've learned something valuable. And, of course, comments about "crazy people" or "nutcases" tell you everything you need to know—maybe not about the company as a whole, but certainly about the person saying them. If you suspect that revealing potentially sensitive information about yourself would make you a target for harassment, it may not be a good idea to disclose your depression.

4. Think about whether performing your job would be more difficult if you disclosed. For example, if you work for the government, would it affect your security clearance? If you work for a day care center, would it make your boss less likely to entrust children to you? If so, consider keeping your diagnosis to yourself.

5. Finally, weigh the pros and cons and make your decision. If you decide you want to disclose, use the process set out in chapter 4 to identify potential accommodations. What kinds of problems does your depression cause you at work? Do you need any accommodations in order to address those problems? What do you need? When will you need it?

I've decided to keep my depression to myself. What are my rights?

You have exactly the same rights as someone without depression, or someone with any other illness that isn't disabling. Employers only have to accommodate disabilities they're aware of. Of course, that doesn't mean your colleagues and supervisor can treat you badly with impunity. You're still protected by your company's internal policies and by whatever state and federal laws apply to general discrimination. But if you don't tell anyone about your depression, you can't turn to the ADA for protection.

I've decided I want to disclose my depression and ask for accommodations, but who should I tell?

The person you most need to tell is whomever would be responsible for negotiating and approving your request or actually providing the accommodation. This is most likely to be your immediate supervisor or manager.

Consider speaking to someone in your company's human resources (HR) department first. Because HR is responsible for retention—that is, finding ways to hang on to good employees—many HR departments devote staff time and energy to making the workplace as comfortable and supportive as possible. If your HR department has a reputation for dealing ethically with employees, going there first will allow you to gather the information and internal support you need in order to have a productive conversation with your boss. A good HR department will be able to tell you what the company has done in similar situations and what you might expect. If your company has never dealt with disability issues before, HR may not be able to give specific help, but at the very least, you should be able to gather some information about what steps to follow to comply with the company's internal procedures. In the best case, HR will take your side and serve as your advocate when management is in the wrong.

When you do speak to HR, stress the need for confidentiality, and follow up your conversation by sending a written note as a reminder. If you have any doubts at all about how your disclosure will be received, make an appointment to discuss it with someone at your company's Employee Assistance Program (EAP) as well. An EAP is required to keep all your information in strictest confidence. EAP employees are often social workers and other health care experts who are better versed in mental health issues than HR staffers, whose expertise lies mostly in hiring, benefits, and training. If your employer includes an EAP in its benefits package, take advantage of the resources it offers. (We'll discuss the role of the EAP in more detail in chapter 7.)

If you don't need an immediate accommodation, but you want to be sure your employer is aware of your disability in case you need one in the future, go to your company's head of HR. If your employer has an Equal Employment Opportunity/Affirmative Action officer, speak to that person as well.

What information do I offer, and how specific do I have to be?

You don't have to give every detail of your diagnosis and treatment. You don't even have to use any special phrases like "ADA" or "reasonable accommodation." You do need to be specific enough for your employer to understand that you have a disabling condition, that your disability affects your ability to do your job, and that something can be done about it. Your employer may ask you to provide proof of your disability, but only as it relates to your ability to do your job.

Who finds out about this information once I've disclosed it?

Your employer is required by law to treat your disclosure and any information related to it (such as your psychiatric history, your diagnosis, and your treatment) as confidential.

The information can't even be kept in the same place as your general personnel file. It has to be stored separately and in a place where only authorized people have access to it.

Your employer is only allowed to share information about your disability with these people: the supervisors and managers who are directly involved in negotiating reasonable accommodations, first aid and safety personnel, and government officials who are investigating ADA claims.

Beyond that, your employer is not allowed to tell anyone—not other managers, not your co-workers, not your customers, *no one*—without your explicit permission. If you want to share the information with other people, you may; otherwise, by law, it goes no further.

Can I ask for what I need without invoking the ADA or even bringing up my depression?

Absolutely! If you have an immediate problem that can be easily resolved, just describe it and ask for the solution you think would be best. Here are some examples:

> *"I'm having a hard time concentrating today, so I'm going to take notes while we talk. Would you mind looking them over afterward to be sure I haven't left out anything important?"*
>
> *"I'm not feeling well this afternoon. Is it all right with you if I leave early and make up for it by staying late tomorrow?"*

Strictly speaking, these statements aren't requests for reasonable accommodation, because they don't link your request to a medical condition or put your employer on notice that you have a disability. On the other hand, there's no reason to turn a small issue into a big one if your problem is easily resolved.

How is that different from an official disclosure under the ADA?

If you want to be a little more specific in order to help a co-worker or boss understand your situation and trigger the protection of the ADA, you have to make it clear that you have a condition that requires accommodation. Again, you don't have to use any special phrases. You can use everyday language to say something like this:

> *"I know we have a policy against letting customers see us eat or drink, but I take medication that makes my mouth really dry. Can I keep a bottle of water with me if I make sure it's out of sight? If that's a problem, maybe I can take shorter but more frequent breaks instead so I can drink something in private."*
>
> *"Starting next Monday, I'm going into the hospital for a serious health problem. I don't know yet how long I'm going to be gone. If I use up my sick time, I'll need to take a leave of absence. Can we meet later today or tomorrow to go over the details?"*

And if you want to be both proactive about your depression and take the opportunity to educate people about it, you can say something that both explains your condition and gives people an opportunity to learn more if they want to.

> *"Sometimes I may seem standoffish, irritable, or distracted. I want you to know that it's not directed at you personally; I have depression and this is just how it affects me sometimes. Please don't be offended."*

"I've been diagnosed with major depression and I'm in the process of getting it under control. Although it may be a little while before I'm a hundred percent again, I am seeing a doctor and following a treatment plan. In the meantime, you should know that I'm having a hard time focusing on long-term goals, so I'd like to work out a plan where we can meet weekly to review my work and identify what I should do next."

"I want you to know that I have depression. I don't expect it to be an issue at work—thanks to good treatment, I haven't had any problems in several years—but I wanted to give you an opportunity to ask me about it if you want to. I've been dealing with this for a long time and I can probably answer any questions you might have."

How can I be sure I don't leave out anything important?

This checklist will help you say everything you need to say, and nothing you don't.

- Describe your disability. You get to decide how general or precise you want to be. Starting at the vague end of the spectrum, you may choose to refer to your depression only in the most general terms: an illness, a medical problem, a disability. You may be slightly more specific and call it a biochemical imbalance or a neurological disorder. To give further detail, you may say that you have a mental illness or a psychiatric disability. Or you might state explicitly that you've been diagnosed with major depression. Again, it's entirely up to you how you want to phrase it.

- Reassure your employer that you're able to perform the main duties of the job. Describe your skills, your credentials, and the successes you've had. Do this *before* talking about any problems you're having. The point is to present your depression as an inconvenience you can overcome with your employer's help, not an insurmountable barrier that will make you more of a drawback than an asset.

- Next, describe the way your depression interferes with your ability to do your work. The more detailed you are in your description, the easier it will be for you to explain why your preferred accommodations will help.

- After that, talk about the accommodations you need and how they'll improve your performance. If you went through the process of brainstorming accommodations as suggested in chapter 4, you should have a list of possibilities as well as the reason why each one would be helpful. Present each one individually, be willing to discuss the pros and cons of each one, and be open to suggestions you may not have thought of. Your employer may not be able to give you everything you want, but you should be able to negotiate an arrangement that works for both of you. (If your employer flatly turns down all your requests and refuses to discuss alternatives, read on to chapter 6, where we discuss what to do about discrimination.)

- Finally, if you think it's necessary, tell your employer where to find more information about your depression and about reasonable accommodations: your doctor or therapist, the Job Accommodation Network (JAN), the local ADA

Disability and Business Technical Assistance Center, or your job coach or rehabilitation counselor if you have one. You can also direct your employer to organizations like the National Depressive and Manic-Depressive Association or the National Alliance for the Mentally Ill for general information about depression. You'll find contact information for these organizations in the appendix.

Can you suggest a good way to word all of this?

Boston University's Center for Psychiatric Rehabilitation suggests this helpful script you can follow:

> *"I'm recovering from (description of your disability). I have/can do (necessary skills and qualifications) to do (main duties of the job), but sometimes (functional limitations) interfere with my ability to (duties you have trouble performing). It would help me to have (name the specific accommodations you need). I work best when (other accommodations). Here's the number of my (therapist, doctor, previous employer, job coach, etc.) for any information you might need about my ability to handle the job."*

You can add the following information, if you want to.

> *"Sometimes you might see (symptoms or behaviors associated with depression). If you notice that, you can (tell the employer what to do)."*

So, for example, if you've realized that you're at your best first thing in the day, you may decide to say something like the following:

"I'm recovering from a medical condition that sometimes affects my energy levels. I can take calls in the twenty-four-hour customer service center and fill out order forms accurately and thoroughly, but in the evening I occasionally get extremely tired and have a hard time focusing my attention. It would help me to take an early shift in the call center rather than a late one. I'd work best if I was here from 6 A.M. to 2 P.M. instead of from 2 P.M. to 10 P.M."

Obviously, you'll insert your own information in the proper places.

Do I have to disclose in person?

No, you can send the appropriate person a letter. Go through the above process to collect your thoughts and present the necessary information in this format, as suggested by JAN.

- Identify yourself as a person with a disability.
- State that you are requesting accommodations under the ADA.
- Identify your specific problematic job tasks.
- Identify your accommodation ideas.
- Request your employer's accommodation ideas.
- Attach medical documentation, if appropriate.
- Ask that your employer respond to your request in a reasonable amount of time. JAN doesn't define how long that would be, but depending on your employer, "reasonable" might be as little as a few days or as much as a month. Certainly, you have the right to expect an answer within no more than six weeks.

Two examples follow on the next pages:

General:

Dear Mr. Boss:

This letter is to inform you that I have a medical condition that qualifies as a disability and that I am requesting accommodation under the Americans with Disabilities Act.

As part of my treatment, I see a doctor at regular times, and must give at least forty-eight hours' notice in order to cancel or reschedule. In the last three months, I've had to miss five mandatory department-wide meetings because they were announced less than twenty-four hours before they happened, giving me no time to reschedule my doctor appointment. I am requesting that these meetings be held on a regular schedule or, alternatively, that I get two or three days' advance notice of meetings whenever possible. This will allow me to plan my schedule around the meetings and ensure my presence.

I have attached a letter from my doctor confirming that my illness is disabling. If you would like further information, please ask. I will provide you with any documentation to which you're legally entitled.

I would appreciate hearing back from you about this request by the end of the month. Thank you for your consideration.

Sincerely,

M. Ployee

Specific:

Dear Mr. Boss:

This letter is to inform you that I am requesting accommodation under the Americans with Disabilities Act for major depression.

Starting my work day at 8 A.M. is extremely difficult for me, as my illness and the medication I take to treat it make me tired and unable to concentrate in the morning. It would help if I could start work later in the day and stay later in the evening, for example, from 11 A.M. to 7:30 P.M. Alternatively, I could work from home on days that you don't need me to be present in the office. I am open to any other ideas you might have that would make it possible for me to perform my job well while accommodating my disability.

I have attached documentation confirming that my depression meets the ADA's definition of disability and documenting my need for reasonable accommodation. If you would like further information, please ask. I will provide you with any documentation to which you're legally entitled.

I would appreciate hearing back from you about this request by the end of the month. Thank you for your consideration.

Sincerely,

M. Ployee

Should I disclose during a job interview?

There are definitely two schools of thought about this issue. On the one hand, disclosing during the interview unmistakably puts the employer on notice that you have a disability the company will have to accommodate once you're hired. On the other hand, it may overshadow your other qualifications and make the employer decide to go with another equally qualified candidate. As always, the choice is up to you.

Leigh Ann, the hospital nurse you met in chapter 3, is re-entering the workforce after taking several months off to focus on her treatment and recovery. After much thought, she's decided to be straightforward about her depression in interviews. "I want employers to know that when I get stressed out, I may have certain needs," she explains. Admitting that she isn't immune to stress is a very big deal indeed in the high-pressure world of medicine, where health care providers are expected to set their own needs aside for the sake of patients. Leigh Ann says she's certain she's missed out on jobs as a result. But, she adds, she'd rather know right away that she and an employer are a bad fit than wait until she's on the job and sliding back into a depressive episode.

What if I need accommodations *for* a job interview?

If you're asking for accommodations during the interview process, speak to the recruiter, the HR representative, or the interviewer (these last two may be the same person). You'll have to offer the same sort of information as you would if you were already on the job: identifying yourself as a person with a disability and providing proof if the employer asks for it.

Accommodations appropriate for a job interview might include scheduling it for your particular "good time of day," interviewing in a quiet room, or being allowed to have a job coach present. You may come up with others to suit your particular needs.

Between hospitalization and other aspects of treatment, I've been out of the workforce for more than a year. How do I explain the gap in my résumé?

Most employers will be understandably curious if you have an unexplained gap in your work history, but their concern is less with what you were doing when you weren't working and more with your fitness for the job. Specifically, they want to know if you were fired for cause, whether you were in jail, or whether for some reason you were unwilling or unable to get a job.

By law, employers are forbidden to ask about your health in a job interview, even if you imply that you were unemployed for health reasons, so if you don't plan to disclose your depression, you may want to say simply that you were taking a medical leave. Of course, since follow-up questions are equally off-limits, the employer may leap to the conclusion that you suffer from some contagious or, worse, terminal illness and choose to go with a healthier candidate. Instead, you may be able to finesse the question by saying that you were taking a sabbatical to pursue personal interests (your mental health is certainly a personal interest!) or taking time off to deal with a family matter (again, your health) which is now resolved. In other words, if you've decided not to disclose your depression, frame your answer in the broadest possible terms with no reference to your health, and then turn the conversation as quickly as possible back to the job you're pursuing and your qualifications for it.

The best way to address a large gap in your résumé

may be not to address it at all, but just to refer to it as "personal time." This does imply, in a way, that you have the financial resources not to *need* a job, so you take the risk that an interviewer will worry that you'll be likely to leave on short notice. That's an issue you can address by emphasizing how very much you're interested in the job in question. You *want* this job and you intend to do it devotedly and well.

Consider this: If you've demonstrated that you have the skills a company needs, you've shown your fervent interest in doing the job the company needs done, and the company chooses not to hire you simply because you chose to devote some personal time to a nonwork pursuit, is this really a company you want to work for?

What's my employer's part in this process?

The ADA requires your employer to accommodate you unless your request is unreasonable—that is, unless it's too expensive or interferes substantially with the employer's ability to do business. That doesn't mean your employer is obligated to give you the exact accommodations you want. You may have to negotiate some other arrangement that accomplishes the goal of helping you get your work done without too much cost or inconvenience.

Some employers are especially sensitive to the needs of people with disabilities and will gladly make the effort to accommodate you. Others may have to be prodded a bit, and you might want to be prepared to answer their questions or send them to other people who can address their concerns. If you think it would help you negotiate, you can even ask an advocate from JAN or a similar organization to talk to your employer about what kinds of accommodations have been helpful and reasonable in similar situations.

As you probably suspect, the more valuable you are to your company, the more you'll be able to ask for. Mark, for example, was considered the most important employee at his company: the first person the founders hired and the driving force behind the firm's main product. He was allowed to retire early, with full-time pay for several months and half-time pay for another year after that. And Leroy had enough clout at his workplace that he was able to take six months off and return to a part-time schedule. If you're in a low-responsibility, high-turnover position, what counts as "reasonable" may be markedly different, and the most you may be able to ask for is a change in hours. But either way, chances are good that your employer just wants to make sure the work gets done.

To repeat something we've already stressed, reasonable accommodations are not special privileges. They're your civil rights.

When is disclosure always the wrong thing to do?

Never, ever try to use your depression as an excuse for bad behavior on the job. If you've been having serious problems at work—coming in late, performing poorly, or having interpersonal problems with your co-workers—address them before things get to the point that you're about to be fired. Yes, your depression may be the cause of your problems. But having a mood disorder doesn't absolve you of the need to take responsibility for your own actions. If you wait until you're called in for a disciplinary meeting, then blurt out that you have a disability and are asking for accommodations under the ADA, it isn't going to come across as proof of your commitment to doing your job well. In fact, it's going to look like a final desperate attempt to get away with something you wouldn't otherwise be able to justify. Your employer will probably respond, "You should have said something sooner. Now you've shown you can't perform the job we hired you to do. It's too late to argue that your problems are due to a disability."

* * *

Although most people will greet your disclosure well, we feel compelled to note that not everyone will—and, surprisingly, the very employers who would seem to be most receptive can turn out to be the least open. A newly minted social worker, Mara was working for a program helping women with drug convictions get clean and regain custody of their children. If any employer should have understood depression and anxiety, hers should have. However, when she disclosed her depression, her supervisor told her that even though she was still performing her job well, she would not receive the promotion she'd earned until she was no longer "in crisis"—an all too common reaction. What if you, too, are treated unfairly because of your depression? We'll discuss what constitutes discrimination, and what you can do about it, in the next chapter.

· 6 ·

Discrimination: The Ugly Truth

Attitudes about depression have changed dramatically in recent years. Once upon a time, no one admitted to having it, never mind being treated for it; the most anyone would say was that someone had "gone away to rest." Today, Prozac is a household word, friends compare therapists over lunch, and memoirs such as William Styron's *Darkness Visible* and Tracy Thompson's *The Beast* have turned illness into literature. At a time when celebrities like newsman Mike Wallace, comedian Drew Carey, economist John Kenneth Galbraith, and musician Bonnie Raitt have all discussed their depression openly, it sometimes seems like everyone is depressed or knows someone who is!

Nonetheless, you've probably run into some harsh stereotypes about depression: the notion that you're either weak, lazy, or just plain faking it, or that you could just "snap out of it" if you tried hard enough; the fear that you might—without warning—turn violent and harm yourself or others; the idea that even after treatment, the slightest amount of stress will make you fall apart.

You may also have encountered other common misconceptions specifically related to work. Maybe someone has told you that because you have a mental illness, your work must be supervised by someone else at all times, or that you'll no longer be allowed to make decisions on your own.

Someone may have suggested that being depressed means you'll never be able to earn an advanced degree or take on responsibilities beyond entry level. If you had to quit or take a leave of absence from a managerial position in order to recover, you may even have been told your career is basically over—that your options are now limited to low-paying, dead-end jobs. And, of course, you're probably concerned that going public with your depression will give your workplace rivals a convenient excuse to look for signs of instability in everything you do.

Lynn was struggling with depression and having a difficult time finding an effective medication. When her boss met with her to complain that her performance was slipping, she decided to reveal her illness, and not long after, she asked for medical leave in order to be briefly hospitalized. Less than a month after she returned, Lynn was fired from the position she'd held for almost a decade. Although she was told her dismissal was merely "a business decision to reduce head count," she soon heard through the grapevine that someone else had been hired to replace her. Faced with this obvious discrimination, Lynn is now seriously considering suing her former employer.

In the decade since the Americans with Disabilities Act became law, most employers have learned about it, and most now try to observe its guidelines to the best of their ability. Nevertheless, it's still a good idea to have a basic idea of your rights and be able to recognize when they're being violated. Some employers may not be aware of the most recent developments in disability law, a field that is constantly changing. Unfortunately, because of the stigma that still surrounds depression or because of the belief that people with disabilities are getting special treatment they don't deserve, some employers are simply unwilling to comply with the law.

One woman we spoke to found out after the fact that the reason she'd been turned down for a job was because one of her references had mentioned in passing that she was taking a common antidepressant. Upon hearing this, she was told, the hiring manager tossed her résumé into the nearest wastebasket, saying, "We don't need any crazies in this company."

In this case, the woman's rights were violated twice: first by the reference who disclosed that she was taking medication, and then by the hiring manager who was clearly denying her an opportunity based on his beliefs about her mental health. Did the reference reveal the woman's medical history accidentally, or under the impression that it would improve her chances of getting the job? Did the hiring manager break the law out of ignorance, or did he know and not care that he was violating the woman's rights? It doesn't matter. The law protects her under all these circumstances.

What qualifies as discrimination?

To put it as simply as possible, an employer is discriminating if he or she treats you at all differently from other employees for reasons unrelated to your ability to do your job well.

To be more specific, the ADA says that people who are disabled and who have the experience and skills to do a job must be given as much of a chance to be hired as any other applicant. Employers also have to treat employees who are disabled the same as any other employee in terms of pay, promotions, raises, training opportunities, benefits, and "other terms or privileges of employment." That means it's *illegal* for employers to do any of the following:

1. Ask you about your health in a job interview. You may

volunteer the information (if, for example, you need reasonable accommodations for the interview), but it's against the law for the employer to broach the subject first, or even to ask follow-up questions if you bring it up in the course of the interview.

2. Use your past employment records, health insurance records, references, or other information for the purpose of finding out whether you have a disability before hiring you.

3. Deny you a job, raise, promotion, benefits, or training for which you have the experience and skills because of your past, present, or potential future mental health and treatment.

4. Deny you a job, raise, promotion, benefits, or training based on the employer's belief that you "can't handle it" because of your depression.

5. Decrease your responsibilities based on your past, present, or future diagnosis or treatment.

6. Refuse to make reasonable accommodations that would help you perform the essential functions of your job.

7. Force you to accept an accommodation, support, or any "special treatment" you haven't requested and don't need.

8. Hold you to different rules and standards than other employees are expected to follow.

9. Fire you for reasons unrelated to your performance.

An employer who contracts with any business, organization, or individual that discriminates is also breaking the law, even if the employer doesn't engage in any discriminatory practices.

And it is absolutely, positively, unquestionably illegal

for employers to retaliate against you or penalize you for exercising your legal rights.

There's a question on my job application form asking me if I've ever seen a psychiatrist. What should I do?

Leave it blank!

Before the ADA became law, many job applications contained this question or one like it. Even high school students applying for jobs at fast food restaurants had to reveal whether they'd ever seen a doctor about depression or anxiety—as though that would disqualify a sixteen-year-old from serving burgers! Today, this question is illegal. Before you're hired, employers may not ask you if you have, or have ever had, a mental illness. They may not ask if you're currently seeing or have ever seen a psychiatrist or therapist. They may not ask you whether you take or have ever taken medication, and they may not ask you what medications you take or have taken.

You may be applying for a position at a company that hasn't updated its paperwork since then and may not be aware that the question is on the application, in which case they may appreciate your pointing it out to them. On the other hand, given that it's been a forbidden question for more than a decade, its presence may be a clue that the company isn't particularly interested in making sure it's abiding by the law, either because it hasn't been paying attention or because it's actively discriminating.

Can an employer require me to undergo a physical exam, drug test, or psychological exam as a condition of being hired?

Employers are allowed to ask about your physical and mental health after they've made you an offer but before you start work, but only if *every* job applicant has to undergo the same exams or tests. You cannot be singled out because of your depression. What's more, if you have to see a health care professional chosen by the employer, the employer is responsible for the related costs. You can't be asked to foot the bill for an exam someone else is requiring you to take in order to be hired.

Be aware that doctor-patient confidentiality does not apply to these types of exams. That doesn't mean you should lie. But if the doctor doesn't tell you clearly what information he or she is going to pass along to your employer, *ask*. You have the right to know.

Can an employer require me to take a psychological exam or ask me about my mental health after I have the job?

Yes, but only if one of these conditions applies:

- If every new hire or current employee is subject to the same treatment. Air Force fighter pilots, for example, all have to pass rigorous psychological tests before they're allowed into the cockpit.

- To confirm that you have a disabling condition. This is allowed only if you've asked for reasonable accommodations and your employer wants proof that you're eligible for them.

- Once you've disclosed a disability, to ensure that it doesn't pose a direct threat to yourself or others. Dolores took a brief leave of absence from her job as an emergency room nurse in order to recover from a depressive episode. Before she was allowed to return to the ER, the hospital where she worked required her to see a therapist who could confirm in writing that she was stable enough to resume her duties.

Because Dolores's work literally placed patients' lives in her hands, the hospital was justified in asking her to undergo psychological evaluation.

Once you're on the payroll, your employer is entitled to ask for expert advice about how your depression affects your ability to perform your job with or without reasonable accommodations. However, your employer does not have the right to know any further details of your diagnosis, health history, or treatment.

I mentioned something about my depression during my job interview, and the employer asked if I needed accommodations under the ADA. Is this legal?

Yes. The EEOC says that if an employer reasonably believes before making a job offer that an applicant will need an accommodation in order to perform the job, the employer *can* ask whether the applicant needs reasonable accommodations and what those accommodations might be. By bringing up your depression, you gave the employer grounds to believe you might need an accommodation. If you don't need accommodations, all you need to say is "no." If you do, it's perfectly all right to ask for them at this point.

Do you suspect your chances of getting the job disappeared the second you admitted to needing accommodations? If an employer asks you if you need them, and you say yes, the employer is not allowed to use that tip-off that you have a disability as an excuse not to hire you.

Can my employer deduct the cost of my reasonable accommodation from my salary?

No. Your employer cannot make up for the cost of providing you with accommodations by decreasing your benefits, denying you a bonus, or paying you less than other people doing the same job. That falls into the category of treating you differently because of your disability.

Your employer has to provide your reasonable accommodations at the company's expense unless the cost of providing the accommodation would be an undue hardship to the business. However, if your accommodation is too expensive for your employer to afford it, you may *choose* to pay for it (or the part of it that poses an undue hardship) yourself. Your employer can't make you pick up the tab, but you have to be given the option to do so voluntarily if that's the only way to make the accommodation possible.

If neither you nor your employer can pay for it, you'll have to come up with another option. Your employer isn't required to give you the best accommodations possible, just accommodations that work.

Can my employer make me work alone or in a different location?

No. You may ask for and receive permission to work from home, in a separate office, or alone as a reasonable accommodation, but your employer can't require you to do so unless it's necessary in order for you to perform the essential duties of your job.

If your employer wants to segregate you from your coworkers in the belief that your depression might make you violent or disruptive, that's discriminatory. Your employer can only isolate or fire you because of a mental illness if it's clear that you pose a direct threat to yourself or others.

Can my employer require me to take antidepressants?

The EEOC has never explicitly addressed this issue, but it has emphasized that the decision to take medication is entirely up to the employee, not the employer. You are the only person responsible for deciding whether or not to take medication. Your employer cannot make that decision for you. Based on this, we believe it's safe to conclude that your employer is not allowed to require you to take medication, either to be hired or to stay employed.

At the same time, being responsible for the decision to take medication also requires you to be responsible for the consequences of not taking it. You can't refuse to do anything about your depression and then argue that your employer shouldn't discipline you for the resulting poor performance or bad behavior. The EEOC makes it clear that as long as your employer is judging you by the same standards as it's judging your co-workers, your employer has the right to invoke whatever company policy applies to employees who don't meet those standards.

Let's say, for example, that as a result of your depression, you have a hard time concentrating and you've been sleeping much more than usual. You've been late for work almost every day in the last two weeks, and you do your duties in a half-hearted way, often leaving them incomplete. Your boss cannot tell you that you'll be fired if you don't start taking medication. On the other hand, your boss can refer you to the part of the company handbook that says employees must show up on time and meet the requirements of their job descriptions in order to remain employed. It's up to you to decide which you prefer: taking medication in the hope of improving your performance, or not taking it at the risk of losing your job.

I need to take a medical leave to get my depression under control. Does my employer have to give me back my job when I return?

Yes. In fact, two separate federal laws—the ADA and the

Family and Medical Leave Act (FMLA)—both say that an employee who takes a medical leave has to be allowed to return to the same job. Furthermore, the ADA says that an employee with a disability who takes a leave of absence as a reasonable accommodation is entitled to return to the same position unless the employer can prove that holding the job open would impose an undue hardship.

If your employer has to fill the position while you're gone, it has to offer you an equivalent vacant position on your return. If an equivalent vacant position isn't available when you come back to work, it has to offer you a vacant position at a lower level.

My employer filled my job while I was away, and there's no equivalent position open right now. I don't want to take the lower-level job my employer is offering me, but if I don't, my employer will let me go. Is this discrimination?

No. The accommodations you ask for have to be reasonable, and the EEOC says it's not reasonable for you to expect to stay out on leave indefinitely rather than take a lower-level position.

In this situation, you have two choices: take the position available to you at the company from which you're on leave, or leave the company to find a better position. Your employer has done its part to accommodate you by offering you what it has. If that's not satisfactory to you, it's time to start circulating your résumé.

My employer has a "no-fault" leave policy under which employees automatically lose their jobs if they've been on leave for more than a certain amount of time. I think my medical leave may last longer than the policy allows. Can my employer let me go?

Not necessarily. Modifying workplace policies is a form of reasonable accommodation. Unless another accommodation would enable you to perform the essential functions of your job, your employer has to modify its policy and allow you to take more time off. The only exception would be if giving you the extra time off would cause your employer an undue hardship, and in order to make that claim, your employer has to take into consideration how much longer you'll be gone. Are you just asking for a few more weeks? Or are you asking your employer to hold a job for you for six months?

Can I be penalized for work I missed during time off that I took as a reasonable accommodation?

Absolutely not. Accommodations are meaningless if you're punished for using them!

Ana works at a department store, selling an upscale brand of cosmetics and skin-care products. Her contract requires her to sell a certain dollar amount of moisturizers and makeup each year in order to keep her job. This year, she's going to miss the mark by several thousand dollars because she took a month of leave as a reasonable accommodation. That doesn't mean the store can fire her for not meeting her sales goals. In fact, her employer will have to take that month of leave into account and make its decision based on her performance the rest of the year.

I didn't get a job because the employer didn't want to offer health insurance. Is this discrimination?

That depends on whether the company offers health benefits to its other employees. The ADA clearly states that employers may not discriminate against otherwise qualified people with disabilities in "privileges of employment," and employer-paid health insurance is without a doubt one of the most valued benefits. (Think of all the people who stick with jobs they hate just because they don't want to lose their insurance coverage.) If an employer pays other employees' insurance premiums but not yours, or offers you a different health plan than it offers other employees, it is treating you differently because of your disability. That's against the law; however, an employer doesn't have to offer you health insurance if it doesn't offer the same benefit to its other employees.

My employer's health care plan excludes pre-existing conditions. That means my medications and therapy aren't covered by insurance, since I was being treated for depression before I took the job. Is this discrimination?

No. The ADA doesn't address pre-existing condition clauses, even though they may have more of a negative effect on you as a person with a disability. The law simply requires your employer to give you access to the same health insurance coverage it offers to all its employees. If no one is offered coverage for pre-existing conditions, there's no discrimination.

If I'm receiving an accommodation and one of my co-workers asks my employer why, can my employer tell my co-workers about my depression?

No. Your depression, treatment, and health history are confidential and cannot be shared without your explicit permission.

As you suspect, this may put your employer in an awkward position if someone asks why you're allowed to work a flexible schedule or where you go for an hour every Thursday afternoon. However, your employer is forbidden to say, or even to imply, that you have a disability. The most your employer may say is that it has legitimate business reasons for its decisions, or that it's acting in compliance with federal law.

If you're concerned about how your co-workers will react to your accommodation, or you're worried that they may consider it a special privilege you don't deserve, you have the option of explaining your depression to them yourself. Go back to chapter 5 and think about the disclosure process as it relates to your co-workers. Although there's always a chance they'll react with teasing, harassment, or other discriminatory behaviors, it's equally possible that they'll be helpful, supportive, and open to learning more.

I think my boss (or a co-worker) is discriminating against me. What should I do?

The first step in resolving any problem is to determine whether you have a valid complaint, or whether there's simply been a misunderstanding. You may want to discuss the situation with your supervisor directly by saying, "I'm concerned that since you learned about my depression, it's influenced your evaluation of my work" or "I'm getting the impression you think my disability is affecting my work, even though my performance clearly shows otherwise."

If you think your employer is offering you accommodations or favors you don't need or want, with the best of intentions, you can say, "I appreciate your offer of (putting my work assignments in writing/giving me a reduced schedule/moving me to another desk), but I'd rather (take my own notes/work a regular schedule/stay where I am). I don't need that kind of accommodation right now. I'll let you know if I need it in the future."

If it seems like your boss or co-workers are treating you with kid gloves in a misguided attempt to be helpful, the Matrix Research Institute suggests this wonderful response: "I know you mean well, but I think you may be underestimating what I can do. If you aren't sure how much I can handle, the best way to find out is to ask me."

Remember, the ADA protects you against discrimination from people who *perceive* your depression as interfering with your ability to do your work, even if you're actually performing well. If you calmly and politely remind people that they should judge you on your abilities, not their fears and stereotypes, that may be all the action you need to take.

I talked to people and nothing changed. What do I do now?

If talking directly to your supervisor or colleagues doesn't seem to make a difference, or if it seems their actions are motivated less by generosity than by malice, your next step is to find out and use your employer's internal policies for dealing with workplace friction. Depending on those policies, you may end up speaking to your supervisor's superior, someone from Human Resources, a counselor at your company's Employee Assistance Program, a union representative, or another designated person responsible for resolving internal issues.

After that, or at the same time, you can turn to an outside advocate for advice and support. This outside advocate may be a professional mentor, family member, or friend who's battled depression and can offer you suggestions based on his or her own experiences. It may be your therapist or psychiatrist. It may be a job coach who is specially trained to come into your workplace to help you communicate with your boss and co-workers and negotiate solutions to problems.

If, after all your best efforts, you still feel you're the victim of discrimination, you can turn to the proper enforcement authority.

To whom do I complain, and how?

The circumstances of your situation determine how and where to make your complaint.

Title I of the ADA

- Has an employer asked you about your mental health during the interview process?

- Has your employer refused to make reasonable accommodations?

- Do you suspect your employer is using your depression as an excuse to discriminate against you in hiring, advancement, firing, compensation, or training—for example, denying you a raise you've earned, refusing you the training you need to advance, or changing your individual benefits package?

These violations fall under Title I of the ADA, which is enforced by the Equal Employment Opportunity Commission. To find the EEOC office nearest you, look in the U.S. government section of your telephone directory, or call 800-669-4000 (voice) or 800-669-6820 (TDD).

You must make your complaint in writing to the EEOC within 180 days (approximately six months) of the discriminatory act in order to launch an investigation. If the agency determines discrimination took place, the EEOC may sue your employer in federal district court. It may also try to negotiate a settlement between you and your employer. Finally, the EEOC may decide not to step in to enforce the law directly, instead sending you a "right to sue" letter allowing you to file a civil lawsuit against your employer yourself.

The EEOC enforces four different laws governing workplace discrimination; in 1999 alone, it received 77,444 complaints, more than 17,000 of them related to the ADA. As a result, the agency often has a substantial backlog. Your case may not come up for several months.

Title III of the ADA

- Have you been kept out of the workplace or segregated to a specific area because of your disability?

- Has your employer refused reasonable modifications to policies, practices, and procedures to accommodate your disability—for example, if you have problems working in an open cubicle surrounded by whirring printers and ringing phones, has your employer refused to let you move to a quieter workstation?

- Have you been unable to take necessary courses and exams because the locations weren't accessible—for example, because you were hospitalized—and your employer refused to help you make alternate arrangements?

Situations like these are covered under Title III of the ADA, which prohibits discrimination by private entities and nonprofit service providers operating public accommodations. To file a complaint under Title III of the ADA, contact the Disability Rights Section of the U.S. Department of Justice's Civil Rights Division within 180 days of the date of the discriminatory act. You may also file a civil lawsuit in federal court without waiting for a "right to sue" letter. For details, call the Department of Justice's ADA information line at 800-514-0301 (voice) or 800-514-0383 (TDD).

The Family and Medical Leave Act

- Has your employer refused to let you take unpaid medical leave?

- Has your employer stopped paying your health benefits while you were on unpaid leave?
- Have you returned to work after an unpaid leave to find your job was gone?

These issues are covered under the FMLA, which requires companies with more than fifty employees to give eligible employees up to twelve weeks of unpaid leave and protects their jobs and health benefits while they're away from work. For information about filing a complaint under the FMLA, contact the Wage and Hour Division of the U.S. Department of Labor at 800-959-3652 or check your local phone book for the Wage and Hour Division office nearest you.

The Rehabilitation Act of 1973
If your disability substantially limits your ability to learn, work, speak, write, walk, see, or hear, and you work in a government office or for an employer that receives federal money, your employer is required to make "appropriate and reasonable" accommodations. If your employer refuses, you can file a complaint under Section 504 of the Rehabilitation Act of 1973. Like Title III of the ADA, the Rehabilitation Act is enforced by the Department of Justice, which you can contact at 800-514-0301 (voice) or 800-514-0383 (TDD).

What do I need to do to prove my case?
The most important thing you can do to bolster your claim is to document it. It's not enough simply to claim you were discriminated against because of your depression; you'll have to show that you were qualified or deserving, that you were turned down for reasons not included in company policy, and that it happened because of bias.

Make a written record of each workplace experience

and interaction you think is evidence of discrimination.

- When did it happen?
- Who was involved?
- Where were you?
- What was said or done?
- How did you react?
- What happened next?
- Was anyone else present?

Try to jot down the pertinent details as soon as possible after they happen, while they're fresh in your memory. In addition, keep copies of relevant paperwork, from memos and performance reviews to the company handbook. If your employer claims you didn't get a raise because of poor performance, you'll have a strong counterargument if you can present proof that you met the written requirements of your job description and that your last three performance reviews were positive.

If an employer is found to be discriminating against me, what's the penalty?

Depending on the circumstances, the employer may be required to hire you, promote you, reinstate you to a position you lost, make up lost back pay, give you a raise, provide you with a reasonable accommodation, or otherwise make you "whole"—that is, in the condition you would have been in if the discrimination hadn't happened. It may also have to pay your attorney's fees, the fees of any expert witnesses called in to testify on your behalf, and any other court costs you incurred.

The EEOC can also assess compensatory damages—that is, make the employer pay you back for actual money lost, for future money lost as a result of the discrimination, and for "mental anguish and inconvenience"—as well as punitive damages if the employer acted with malice or reckless indifference. However, the employer won't have to pay damages if it can prove it tried in good faith to provide you with reasonable accommodations.

In addition, the employer may have to post notices informing all employees that it violated the law and advising them of their rights. The employer may also be required to identify the source of the discrimination, take action to cure it and minimize its chances of happening again, and stop the specific discriminatory practices you experienced.

None of your examples in this chapter seem to fit my situation.

We've tried to bring up some of the more common questions and concerns about discrimination. If you want to talk about the specifics of your own circumstances, or if you're not sure whether you have a valid complaint, call the EEOC at 202-663-4691. An EEOC lawyer will interpret and explain the ADA and other laws against workplace discrimination—for just the cost of a phone call to Washington, D.C. What a bargain!

Is it true that I'll never be able to get a good job again?

Absolutely not! A recently completed study by Boston University's Center for Psychiatric Rehabilitation clearly indicates that people with mental illness (including not just major depression, but conditions such as schizophrenia) can still have responsible, rewarding, meaningful careers. After talking to almost 500 people working in a wide range of careers, the researchers came to the following conclusions:

- While you may have to work harder than the average person to reach your professional goals, they aren't automatically out of reach just because you've been diagnosed with a major mental illness. Depression doesn't have to stand between you and a full-time job, an advanced degree, increased responsibility, or a salary you can live on.

- Being treated for depression doesn't limit your choice of career fields. Of course, it's common for people who have used mental health services to take jobs in mental health self-help and advocacy organizations, but people with psychiatric disabilities are successful in any number of fields, from health and social services to technology, marketing, sales, and education.

- Depression won't necessarily keep you out of a corner office. Almost 20 percent of the study's participants were at the "executive level"—CEOs and company presidents—and another large percentage were middle managers.

Hold your head high, and stand up to discrimination if you encounter it. Even if you've decided that downshifting your career, changing jobs, or switching to a part-time schedule is best for your health, that says nothing about your skills, your intelligence, or your ability to support yourself.

· 7 ·

Getting the Help You Need

Although Meg could hold herself together in groups, she was out of control in one-on-one situations, either bursting into tears or unable to speak at all. She knew her co-workers were starting to talk about her unusual behavior, but she was more afraid to get professional help for her depression than she was to cry at her desk. She didn't know where to begin, and she was convinced everyone at work would find out her deepest fears and secrets.

Both in our daily lives and while researching this book, we've encountered a disturbing number of people who knew they were depressed but refused to seek out help. They often said they were worried that using the health benefits available to them through work would entitle their employers to information that could be used against them. In discussing the resources available to you, we hope to allay your anxieties with a realistic look at what you can expect in the way of affordability, confidentiality, and appropriate treatment.

What resources are available to me through my employer?

That depends on your employee benefits. If your benefits package includes a health plan, it may cover a certain number of appointments with a therapist, psychiatrist, or other mental health professional; check with your insurer for details.

How do I find treatment, and how much can I expect to pay?

As with any kind of health care, your costs will depend on your insurance coverage. Check your insurance information to find out what your provider charges and what conditions it places on coverage. Some health plans will only cover your treatment if you choose your doctor or therapist from a pre-approved list, while others will let you choose your own provider. Your payment method will also depend on your health plan; you may pay as little as a $10 co-pay, or you may have to pay the therapist's full fee up front and file a claim for later reimbursement.

If your insurance doesn't cover mental health care, or if you're paying out of pocket for any other reason, therapy may cost you anywhere from $50 to $300 an hour depending on where you live and the therapist's credentials. If money is an issue, look into clinics run by public hospitals or local mental health associations, which often set their fees on a sliding scale based on clients' income. Some private therapists may be willing to negotiate a lower fee, as well.

In most cases, speaking to an Employee Assistance Program (EAP) counselor will cost you nothing; however, you'll probably be limited to a specific number of appointments.

I've found a therapist I like, but my insurance will only cover fifteen sessions a year. Should I even bother going?

Absolutely. Depending on how well you respond to therapy and what your treatment involves, you may not even need that many sessions to launch your recovery. You also have the option of continuing to see the therapist at your own expense after the fifteen covered sessions are up.

I don't like the therapist my health plan sent me to. What can I do?

Therapy won't work if you don't like and trust your therapist. If you don't think you can work with the therapist you're sent to, ask for another referral, and keep doing it until you find a good fit. Alternatively, you may want to choose your own therapist and pay for your appointments yourself.

If I lose my job, change jobs, or get divorced, do I lose the health care coverage that's paying for my treatment?

Not necessarily. A federal law called the Consolidated Omnibus Budget Reconciliation Act, or COBRA, may let you, your spouse, and your dependent children extend your existing coverage under your employer's plan for up to eighteen months after leaving the job. You will have to pay 100 percent of the premium, which is usually considerably more than you were paying before, but generally less than you would have to pay to get insurance on your own. You can get more information about COBRA from your health plan.

Also, consider contacting your state government to find out whether you and your family may be eligible for public health insurance.

Will having a record of treatment for depression keep me from getting new insurance if I lose mine?

If you've lost your health insurance, either because you've left your job or for some other reason, you're probably worried about finding a new health plan that will cover your treatment. Under certain circumstances, the Health Insurance Portability and Accountability Act of 1996 (HIPAA) may help you.

HIPAA is quite limited. It applies only to people who were most recently covered by a group health plan (in other words, no one who has *individual* insurance coverage) and who have had continuous health insurance coverage for the previous eighteen months. It does *not* require employers to offer or pay for health coverage, guarantee health insurance for everyone, cap the amount insurers can charge, prohibit all exclusions of pre-existing conditions, require group health plans to offer specific benefits, or guarantee you the right to keep the same coverage when you move from one job to another.

However, HIPAA *does* limit the circumstances under which an insurer can use your pre-existing condition as a reason to turn you down for coverage. It also says group health plans cannot refuse to cover your pre-existing condition or charge you more than other plan members. And finally, it guarantees that as long as you meet certain guidelines, you will be able to buy health insurance if you lost yours when you left a job and have no other coverage.

What's the Mental Health Parity Act and how does it affect me?

The Mental Health Parity Act of 1996 (MHPA) says that group health plans, insurance companies, and HMOs that offer mental health coverage cannot set lower annual or lifetime dollar limits on mental health benefits than it does on medical and surgical benefits. Here are some examples:

- If your insurer says that over your lifetime, it will cover up to $1 million in medical and surgical care, but only $100,000 in mental health care, it may be violating the law.

- If your group health plan says it will cover mental health appointments only if they cost $75 or less, but puts no such limits on medical or surgical care, it may be violating the law.

MHPA only applies to group health plans with more than fifty workers. It doesn't prevent insurance providers from limiting mental health coverage in other ways, such as requiring higher co-pays or limiting the number of visits covered. It also doesn't require health plans to offer mental health benefits; it only applies to plans that already do. However, it's a first step toward recognizing that depression and other mental health issues are no less important and worthy of treatment than broken bones or infections.

Health insurance law in the United States is extremely complex and changes often, and there's no way for us to cover it all in the scope of this chapter. We've listed some resources in the appendix that will help you find the most up-to-date details.

What is an EAP and what can it do for me?

As part of their benefits package, many employers give their employees access to a service called an Employee Assistance Program, or EAP. An EAP is essentially a group of professional counselors whose job it is to help you with personal and professional problems—from conflict with co-workers to trouble finding child care—before they become serious enough to interfere with your ability to do your job. Your company contracts with an EAP provider, which employs these counselors much as an HMO employs doctors.

To use the EAP to connect with mental health services, just call the EAP's appointment line and explain why you're calling, what services you think you need, and where you're located. You'll get a referral to a conveniently located counselor, whom you'll be able to see a number of times (the exact number will vary based on your company's plan). If the counselor can't help you resolve your problems within the allotted number of appointments, you'll be able to get a referral to an outside therapist, psychiatrist, or other appropriate provider.

EAP services are a huge bargain—in fact, most of the time, they'll cost you absolutely nothing! If you have access to an EAP through your employee benefits package, by all means, take advantage of it—it's the easiest way to take your first step toward mental health care.

How much of what I tell the EAP counselor will get back to my boss or co-workers?

EAP services are intended to be strictly confidential. In some cases, if your boss has asked you to see an EAP counselor to deal with workplace issues, the counselor will have to inform your boss that you're coming to appointments as required, but your boss is not entitled to know the details.

Employers offer EAP services to head off employee problems at minimal expense. If no one wants to go to the EAP because they're afraid their lives will become an open book, they'll end up getting treatment through their health insurance plan, which costs the employer more. So it's in the EAP's best interest to maintain a spotless reputation. If you're concerned, ask around a bit. Without going into detail, mention to a few co-workers that you're curious just how much they trust the EAP to keep sensitive information private. If they've had a bad experience, they'll probably be eager to tell you about it.

How can my company's EAP
help me find a therapist?

The EAP will have a list of providers in your area who are part of your health plan. Instead of opening the yellow pages and choosing a psychologist or counselor at random, you can ask your EAP counselor for referrals. Since your EAP counselor already knows you and has a sense of your questions and concerns, you're more likely to be sent to someone who suits your needs.

"I like my EAP counselor even better than the psychiatrist she referred me to," said Claire, whom you'll learn more about in chapter 8. "I've actually gone back to her a few times rather than seeing the psychiatrist."

I've found treatment through my employee
benefits package. Is my employer entitled
to know anything about my depression?

It's extremely unusual for an employer to have a *right* to access your medical information. If you're applying for a job that requires a thorough background check—for example, law enforcement or security, or a government job requiring security clearance—you'll probably have to sign a release giving the employer access to your health care records. You may also have to release your medical records if you're suing your employer in civil court. Other than that, your employer has no right to know anything beyond the fact that you're using your health benefits. Unfortunately, that doesn't mean it's impossible for details to get out.

How is that possible if my doctor is required to
keep my treatment confidential?

The concept of doctor-patient confidentiality is enshrined in medical ethics, but in reality, there's no way to guarantee that your medical records are absolutely confidential.

Many insurance companies, managed health care organizations, and HMOs demand that your doctors give them detailed information about your diagnosis and your health history before they'll authorize payment. Some employers, as we've already noted, will insist on a thorough background check. Someone without access to your records may overhear an authorized person talking about them. Although your doctor can only discuss your health if you have given consent or if forced to by a court order, there are dozens of other ways your mental health records might be distributed, examined, and reviewed beyond your therapist's or psychiatrist's office. In a May 1994 article about health care confidentiality, for example, *Wall Street Journal* reporter Ellen Schultz mentions an EAP consultant who called a managed-care facility to ask about a woman's records. Without determining whether the consultant had the right to the information or even asking for the consultant's identity, the person at the facility reportedly accessed the files and said, "Hmm . . . I see here that she's depressed. No wonder. She had that hysterectomy two years ago."

What's more, as the cost of health care goes up and employers become more insistent about keeping expenses down, insurers are computerizing and centralizing their records as a way of cutting costs. You may have heard of the Medical Information Bureau (MIB), a nationwide database of health care claims. (Insurers have used these records to withhold coverage—for example, denying disability insurance or life insurance to people who have been treated for depression on the grounds that someone with a history of mental illness is more likely to be unable to work, to die young, or even to commit suicide.) If you've signed a release giving access to your records as a condition of a job interview, your health care claims are an open book to supervisors, HR managers, and possibly even recruiters and employment screening agencies. Anyone with access to your records in the MIB can see what conditions you've been treated for, when, and by whom. What's stopping them from discriminating against you as a result of what they learn? Only the possibility that you'll find out and sue them.

So how do I keep my mental health history as private as possible?

The only way to be certain that your records remain private is to pay for your therapy and medication entirely out of your own pocket rather than getting it through your health care plan. If you aren't filing insurance claims, there's no record of your treatment in the MIB.

For many, paying the full cost of therapy and medications is not an option. Therefore, carefully read any release you're asked to sign, especially when you're taking a new job or joining a new insurance plan at your current job. You may even want to have a lawyer review any employment agreements you're about to sign to ensure your privacy is protected. You may also want to tell your therapist in writing that you do not wish to have your records released for review by anyone without your explicit written permission. This will obligate your therapist to contact you any time anyone approaches him or her about your records. You'll know not only who's asking, but what they want to know.

***

Although we've tried in this chapter to alert you to the possibility that your treatment won't be entirely confidential and may be expensive, we certainly don't intend to frighten you away from it. For one thing, it's entirely possible to find treatment that's both effective and affordable. What's more, the truth is that your boss and co-workers are unlikely to find out about your depression unless you tell them. Besides, we would no more suggest you avoid getting help for your depression for the sake of confidentiality or frugality than we would suggest someone with cancer skip chemotherapy.

We understand and empathize with your concerns. We also believe *nothing is more important than recovery.* Depression is a life-threatening illness; it's your right to fight it with dignity and recover from it without shame.

· 8 ·

What Depression Can Teach You

Depression lowers our standards, making us believe we simply don't have what it takes to succeed—in work, in love, in life. It may seem too difficult to do more than the least we can do to get by. We grossly underestimate ourselves, we put ourselves in circumstances that only reinforce our feelings of being inadequate, our self-esteem slumps, and we shrink our expectations even further. And around and around we go, digging ourselves deeper by the day. Does this sound familiar?

And yet the spiral leads up as well as down. Learning to live with a mood disorder can actually lead you to more fulfillment, more satisfaction, and even a greater sense of achievement. "Impossible!" we hear you exclaim. After all, what could possibly be positive about a chronic, progressive, and widely stigmatized illness? Still, quite a few people who have faced and fought off depression say the experience taught them valuable lessons, both large and small. In some cases, it motivated them to make major life changes they'd never dreamed were possible.

Claire: "I feel like I have more power."

By the time Claire reached her late teens, she had decided that while she could eke out tiny morsels of pleasure by smoking pot or following her favorite band on tour, being unhappy was normal and only to be expected. That's just the way life was.

She spent her twenties drifting from one short-term administrative position to another. Relying on temporary employment agencies for job placements meant she never had to send out résumés or go on interviews, never had to commit to anything long-term, and never had to give more than a moment's notice if she felt like moving on. "After six months anywhere, I would start panicking because I felt so stuck," she explained. "I didn't know I was depressed, I just thought the next job, the next town, the next *whatever* would be better."

Over time, though, Claire realized the true cost of her so-called freedom: she had thousands of dollars in credit card debt, no savings, and no health insurance. She was living paycheck to paycheck, not making enough to meet her expenses but feeling powerless to do anything that might improve her finances. The idea of actually looking for a job was "just too hideous to contemplate." If she set a goal of finding satisfying work, she was admitting she cared, and if she admitted she cared, she was leaving herself open to the possibility that she might fail—something she thought was likely, since she had no confidence in her intelligence or skills, and no idea what she might actually enjoy or want to do. By not trying to do better, she was at least avoiding doing worse.

Nonetheless, she managed to leverage her years of administrative experience into a position as a departmental secretary at a state university. She now says that's the decision that started her trip back up the spiral. It didn't seem that way at first, of course. In the beginning, she was able to do her work with, as she says, "one brain tied behind my back." Then she began to feel "scattered, frazzled, stressed, unfocused, teary." She sat at her desk playing computer solitaire and sending instant messages to her online friends, letting basic tasks pile up. When she began to have anxiety attacks at the thought of going to the office and found herself spending part of each day hiding in the bathroom for fear someone would confront her about the work she was leaving undone, she realized she was suffering from something more severe than boredom.

Fortunately, for the first time in her life, she was working someplace where help was available through her employee benefits package. She contacted the university's EAP for information about finding a therapist and got a mid-day appointment. After worrying briefly about how to explain her need to leave the office, Claire decided she had nothing to lose by being open. Her office was in charge of employee orientation, after all, and she herself had photocopied the ADA information sheet given to every new hire. Besides, she thought, her boss might imagine something worse if she left the reason for her absence to his imagination. She sent him an e-mail saying she needed regular time off during the week in order to be treated for depression.

Working with both a counselor and a psychopharmacologist, Claire decided to commit herself to recovery, whatever it took. She remembers holding her first prescription for antidepressants in her hand and thinking, "Imagine if this actually works. Imagine if this paralysis lifts and I have energy again."

Just a few weeks later, she found herself facing a stubborn problem at work. In the past, she would have avoided dealing with it as long as possible. This time, she was able to tackle it with the kind of focus and creativity that let her improvise a solution. She thought it was a fluke. It wasn't.

Over the next few months, Claire was delighted to find she was looking forward to seeing friends after work rather than rushing home to her bed. A death in her family left her deeply sad, but not overwhelmed. For the first time in years, she signed up for an exercise class at the university's gym. She began taking on more responsibility at work. She even started applying for other jobs with more interesting duties and better pay.

It's been two years since Claire, now thirty-one, started treatment. Ask her how her life has changed since then, and she exclaims enthusiastically, "How *hasn't* it?" She's gotten a promotion and a raise. She's also lost fifty pounds, quit smoking, moved to a better neighborhood, and begun working with a credit counselor to get her finances in order. What's more, she's thinking of using the tuition breaks given to university employees to pursue the advanced degree she gave up on years ago. And in a development that would have been unimaginable for "the old Claire," she's chosen to separate from her husband until he stops drinking and begins treatment for his own years-long depression—and, acknowledging that his decision is out of her hands, she's begun to date again. It's time, she says, to start thinking about what she wants to do with her life.

"I feel like someone flipped a switch in my brain that had been off for a long time," she said recently. "I no longer have that aura of desperation."

Mark: "I finally get to do things I want to do."

Mark, a research scientist, had spent most of his career at one company, joining it so early in its existence that he did a bit of everything—computer programming, electronics, technical writing, employee training. He'd even taken out the trash now and then, back when there were only eight employees. After 23 years, the company had grown to more than 400 people, and he'd risen to the top of his department. He was the top employee after the founders themselves, a stockholder, the kind of person other employees turned to for advice. The only problem was that he was, frankly, miserable.

Mark believes his depression was triggered when his family moved from an inner suburb, close to the city and convenient to public transportation, to the kind of distant community where the nearest supermarket is five miles away and no one ever gets out of the car. His commute doubled, his contact with people outside work dropped to almost nothing, and he sank deep into isolation, coming home from work only to eat dinner and head straight to bed. On weekends, he lay in bed all day listening to National Public Radio, emerging just long enough to visit the kitchen for an occasional meal.

Unlike many people, Mark recognized what he was experiencing as a depressive episode. He'd first been diagnosed with major depression in the early 1970s and had spent many years working with therapists and trying a multitude of medications, with varying degrees of success. This, however, was the first time he was too depressed to function at work. Instead, he spent hours sitting at his desk either surfing the Web or simply staring at the ceiling. It was obvious something was wrong; he didn't want to try to hide it any longer. He went to his boss, one of the top executives, and told him he was having problems concentrating and wasn't getting anything done.

What happened next shocked him. "Even though I'd been working with him for twenty years, he never said another word to me about it, just sent over someone from human resources," he recalled, an indignant edge beneath his otherwise calm tone. "They said they wanted to work out a better schedule for me, but we eventually 'came to an agreement' that I would leave."

In the end, Mark's employers agreed to pay him a generous severance package. In exchange, he agreed to walk away without argument from a company he'd helped build.

At first, he was bitter and resentful that the people with whom he'd worked so closely for so long were so willing to show him the door. But the more he thought about it, the more it became clear that he hadn't been happy at the company for a long time. He realized that the only reason he'd pursued a career in science at all was for the income potential, and that he would have been much happier if he'd gone into a more people-oriented field, even if it had meant less money.

Mark decided to invest several months in exploring his skills and preferences so he wouldn't make the same mistake twice. Before long, he hit on a job that perfectly combined his people skills and his scientific experience: leading physics labs at a local college. Although he's finding that teaching is harder and more time-consuming than he'd anticipated, he enjoys the respect he gets from his students and colleagues, the intellectual stimulation of the work, and the excitement of feeling that he's making a contribution to the next generation of research. After more than a year sunk in deep depression, Mark attributes his recovery not only to aggressive treatment, but to his new career.

"I think without the depression, I probably would have had a completely different career," he mused. "My first therapist was helpful, but I think he could have encouraged me to try other things rather than trying to teach me to be happier where I was."

Fawn: "The experience of depression changed my career forever."

As you may have realized by now, this book was inspired to some extent by my own experiences. One morning in January 1995, I plummeted into my first—and, I hope, last—episode of major depression. I was constantly on the verge of tears, prone to sobbing uncontrollably at innocuous things like detergent commercials. I was exhausted, unable to fall asleep until after midnight and inevitably snapping awake again at 4 A.M. I couldn't focus on simple tasks without talking myself, out loud, through each step: "Pick up the phone. Push the 7. Push the 3. Push the 8." I felt raw, stupid, helpless.

In a sense, I was in an ideal situation to cope with the effects of a depressive episode. Self-employed and working from a home office, I didn't need to present an upbeat, competent face to the world for eight or more hours a day; in fact, I did most of my work by phone and e-mail and rarely needed to see clients or colleagues at all. I was able to work at my own speed, on my own time, with frequent breaks when I needed them. But I still had appointments to make, obligations to meet, projects to complete, and a professional reputation to uphold—and I could barely manage to take a shower each morning.

I couldn't put together a grocery list, never mind a coherent paragraph. I sat at my computer playing solitaire or just staring out the window, trying hard not to think about my deadlines and the increasingly annoyed messages on my voice mail. I was in no shape to drum up new business. I couldn't even keep up with the work I already had. I was terrified that I was destroying my career. What was I going to tell clients when I called to ask them for more time to do their work? How would I explain the deadlines I'd already missed? What good is a writer who can't write?

Luckily, I had a safety net: a therapist who with utmost gentleness told me she thought it was time to consider my mood a medical issue. After five weeks of antidepressants and intense weekly therapy appointments, my depression began to lift, and within a few more weeks,

I was looking forward to writing again.

The most difficult part of my recovery was the day I forced myself to call all my clients to say I needed extensions on my deadlines. I'd planned a little speech about having been seriously ill but now recovering, but to my relief, instead of asking me for an explanation, everyone just told me to get well soon. In truth, it took me another three months to catch up—but by the end of that time, I was astonished by how energetic and productive I'd become. I felt better than I'd felt for the better part of a decade, better than what I'd come to believe was "fine." It was my first hint that I'd probably been mildly to moderately depressed for quite a while.

Instead of wanting to put it behind me, I became fascinated by the strategies people develop in order to function in spite of depression. I wrote an article about depression in the workplace for the *Boston Herald*. I worked on a Web site for Boston University's Center for Psychiatric Rehabilitation about accommodating mental illness at work and at school. There was plenty of information available, but it was so difficult to find, and even more difficult to understand. If I was struggling to grasp it, even though I was an experienced researcher and back to my normal self, how hard must it be for people to make sense of it when they needed it most?

At the same time, my acquaintanceship with Beth—a journalist writing about careers and a management consultant willing to be a source of information—was evolving into mutual support and friendship between two outspoken self-employed women. As we talked one day over coffee about her experiences working with employees in troubled workplaces, I found myself asking her, "How would you feel about writing a book with me about depression and work?"

And here it is.

***

Being treated for depression won't make life magically simple or perfect. Claire still isn't sure what she wants to do when she grows up. Mark is wrestling with a troubled marriage. We all have our share of difficult family members, frustrating co-workers, demanding friends, overbearing bosses. The difference is that depression enables us to acknowledge our limitations and work with them rather than fighting them by pretending they don't exist. More importantly, recovering from depression frees us to exercise our precious right and ability to make choices.

Don't think of depression as an unconquerable barrier to your happiness and success; it may actually be the wake-up call you need to start identifying the choices you want to make. We can choose to discover the environment and people who nurture our talents, our desires, our goals, and our dreams. And that's the key to building not just a rewarding career, but a satisfying life.

• Appendix •

Resources for More Information on Depression and Your Rights As a Depressed Employee

Government Agencies

Disability and Business Technical Assistance Centers (DBTACs)
Phone/TTY: 800-949-4232
Web: www.adata.org

Ten DBTACs across the country offer ADA information, technical assistance, training, materials, and referrals to the public, with special attention to the needs of small businesses. They're funded by the National Institute on Disability and Rehabilitation Research (NIDRR), part of the U.S. Department of Education. The toll-free number will automatically connect you to the center nearest you. You can also contact your regional DBTAC directly.

Region 1 (Conn., Maine, Mass., N.H., R.I., Vt.)
New England DBTAC
Adaptive Environments Center, Inc.
374 Congress Street, Suite 301
Boston, MA 02210
Phone/TTY: 617-695-1225
Web: www.adaptenv.org/neada

Region 2 (N.J., N.Y., P.R., V.I.)
Northeast DBTAC
Cornell University Program on Employment and
Disability
107 ILR Extension Building
Ithaca, NY 14853-4901
Phone: 607-255-8348
TTY: 607-255-2891
Web: www.ilr.cornell.edu/ped/daa/dbtac.html

Region 3 (Del., D.C., Md., Pa., Va., W. Va.)
Mid-Atlantic DBTAC
ADA Information Center for the Mid-Atlantic Region
451 Hungerford Drive, Suite 607
Rockville, MD 20850
Phone/TTY: 301-217-0124
Web: www.adainfo.org

Region 4 (Ala., Fla., Ga., Ky., N.C., S.C., Miss., Tenn.)
Southeast DBTAC
UCP National Center for Rehabilitation Technology
at Georgia Tech
490 Tenth Street
Atlanta, GA 30318
Phone/TTY: 404-385-0636
Web: www.sedbtac.org

Region 5 (Ill., Ind., Mich., Minn., Ohio, Wis.)
Great Lakes DBTAC
University of Illinois/Chicago
Department on Disability & Human Development
1640 West Roosevelt Road, M/C 626
Chicago, IL 60608
Phone/TTY: 312-413-1407
Web: www.adagreatlakes.org

Region 6 (Ark., La., N. Mex., Okla., Tex.)
Southwest DBTAC
Independent Living Research Utilization
2323 South Shepherd Boulevard, Suite 1000
Houston, TX 77019
Phone/TTY: 713-520-0232
Web: www.ilru.org/dbtac

Region 7 (Iowa, Kans., Mo., Nebr.)
Great Plains DBTAC
ADA Project
University of Missouri/Columbia
100 Corporate Lake Drive
Columbia, MO 65203
Phone/TTY: 573-882-3600
Web: www.adaproject.org

Region 8 (Colo., Mont., N. Dak., S. Dak., Utah, Wyo.)
Rocky Mountain DBTAC
Rocky Mountain ADA Technical Assistance Center
3630 Sinton Road, Suite 103
Colorado Springs, CO 80907
Phone/TTY: 719-444-0268
Web: www.ada-infonet.org

Region 9 (Ariz., Calif., Hawaii, Nev., Pacific Basin)
Pacific DBTAC
Public Health Institute
2168 Shattuck Avenue, Suite 301
Berkeley, CA 94704-1307
Phone: 510-848-2980
TTY: 510-848-1840
Web: www.pacdbtac.org

Region 10 (Alaska, Idaho, Oreg., Wash.)
Northwest DBTAC
Washington State Governor's Committee on
Disability Issues & Employment
P.O. Box 9046
Olympia, WA 98507-9046
Phone/TTY: 360-438-4116
Web: www.wata.org/NWD

National Institute of Mental Health (NIMH)
6001 Executive Boulevard, Rm. 8184, MSC 9663
Bethesda, MD 20892-9663
Phone: 301-443-4513
Web: www.nimh.nih.gov

NIMH is part of the National Institutes of Health, the U.S. government's main biomedical and behavioral research agency. It conducts research and clinical trials in locations across the country. If you need information about depression, its current treatments, recent research, and trials of experimental medications, this is a good place to begin. You may be particularly interested in NIH Publication No. 96-3919, a free brochure about what supervisors can do when an employee is depressed.

U.S. Department of Justice
950 Pennsylvania Ave. NW
Civil Rights Division
Disability Rights Section-NYAVE
Washington, DC 20530
Phone: 800-514-0301
TTY: 800-514-0383
Web: www.usdoj.gov/crt/ada/adahom1.htm

The Department of Justice enforces antidiscrimination laws, including the Americans with Disabilities Act, by conducting investigations, litigating violations, and ensuring that settlements and consent decrees are carried out. Call for general ADA information and answers to technical questions, to order free ADA materials, or to ask about filing a complaint.

U.S. Equal Employment Opportunity Commission (EEOC)
1801 L Street, NW
Washington, DC 20507
Phone: 800-669-4000
TTY: 800-669-6820
Web: www.eeoc.gov

The EEOC enforces most federal laws prohibiting employment discrimination. If you suspect you're being treated unfairly at work because of your depression, call the toll-free number to be connected automatically to the nearest EEOC district office.

Other Agencies and Organizations

American Psychological Association
750 First Street NE
Washington, DC 20002-4242
Phone: 202-336-5510 or 800-374-2721
Web: www.apa.org

With more than 159,000 members, the APA is the largest association of psychologists not just in the United States, but in the world. In addition to training professionals and conducting public education programs, it maintains a therapist referral service that will direct you to qualified professionals in your area. The APA also operates PsycPORT.com, a huge online index of current news about psychology and mental health.

Job Accommodation Network (JAN)
West Virginia University
P.O. Box 6080
Morgantown, WV 26506-6080
Phone/TTY: 800-526-7234
Web: janweb.icdi.wvu.edu

Funded in part by the President's Committee on Employment of People with Disabilities, JAN is a nonprofit organization that offers free advice about reasonable accommodations in the workplace. Its toll-free hot line operates Monday through Friday during business hours. In addition, the JAN Web site features a database of accommodations people have used successfully, as well as hundreds of links to sites about employment, discrimination, government agencies, and related resources.

Judge David L. Bazelon Center for Mental Health Law
1101 15th Street NW, Suite 1212
Washington, DC 20005-5002
Phone: 202-467-5730
TTY: 202-467-4232
Web: www.bazelon.org

The nonprofit Bazelon Center works with local, state, and national advocacy groups to defend the rights of people with mental illnesses and developmental disabilities. It also offers advice to other lawyers and produces a variety of publications explaining key legal and policy issues in everyday language. The Bazelon Center does not handle individual requests from the public for information and assistance; however, its Web site is full of useful information. In particular, look for the pages about how the ADA applies to people with psychiatric disabilities and how the law is currently being interpreted. When the law changes—which it does, fairly often—Bazelon Center lawyers update the site to reflect the most recent decisions and explain them in terms that are relatively easy to understand.

Consumer Organizations

National Alliance for the Mentally Ill
Colonial Place Three
2107 Wilson Blvd., Suite 300
Arlington, VA 22201-3042
Phone: 703-524-7600
TTY: 703-516-7227
NAMI HelpLine: 800-950-NAMI (800-950-6264)
Web: www.nami.org

NAMI is a leader in the fight to end the stigma and discrimination directed at people with severe mental illness (including depression and bipolar disorder). It focuses on self-help and support for the mentally ill and their families. In addition to its public education programs, NAMI is also politically active, lobbying at the local, state, and national levels for increased funding for research, adequate health insurance, rehabilitation, housing, and employment.

National Depressive and Manic-Depressive Association
730 N. Franklin Street, Suite 501
Chicago, IL 60610-7204
Phone: 312-642-0049 or 800-826-3632
Web: www.ndmda.org

Founded in 1978, NDMDA has roughly 30,000 members in more than 200 local chapters. It's dedicated to education, support, and self-help for people with mood disorders and their friends and family. Behind all of the organization's work is its view of depression and bipolar disorder as treatable biological illnesses. NDMDA sponsors conferences and lectures and publishes newsletters and books.

Research Institutions

Boston University Center for Psychiatric Rehabilitation
940 Commonwealth Avenue West
Boston, MA 02215
Phone: 617-353-3549
TTY: 617-353-7701
Web: www.bu.edu/cpr

The Center for Psychiatric Rehabilitation is a leading academic institution in the field of psychiatric rehabilitation—that is, in helping people with mental illness become and remain part of the mainstream both professionally and socially. In addition to extensive research, it offers professional training to mental health personnel as well as career coaching and counseling services to consumers. You can also sign up to participate in one of the Center's many research projects. Don't miss the Center's Web site on handling psychiatric disabilities at work and at school, located online at www.bu.edu / cpr / jobschool.

Matrix Research Institute
100 North 17th Street
Robert Morris Building, 10th Floor
Philadelphia, PA 19103
Phone: 215-569-2240
TDD: 215-569-8098
Web: www.matrixresearch.org

MRI develops programs and practices that help people with serious mental illnesses enter and remain in the workplace. You may be especially interested in its "mental illness and work" brochure series, a $50 set of fifteen pamphlets specifically designed to help people with psychiatric disabilities of all sorts make work a priority in their lives. In addition to information about your rights in the workplace, the series discusses important basic information: why work is important, how to develop a résumé, how to apply and interview for jobs, and how to prepare to start work.

Online Resources

Dr. Ivan's Depression Central
www.psycom.net/depression.central.html

This site is packed with useful links hand-selected by New York psychiatrist and psycho-pharmacologist Ivan Goldberg, a former staff member of the National Institute of Mental Health and a faculty member at Columbia University. Dr. Goldberg, who specializes in working with people who have treatment-resistant mood disorders, points you to an astonishing range of information. Whether you're looking for pharmaceutical trials, the latest thinking on treatment strategies, information about depression in specific groups, or hints for speeding your recovery, you'll find it here, along with a powerful, flexible search engine to help you find specific nuggets of data you might not otherwise be able to track down.

FirstGov for Workers

www.workers.gov

If you're in the United States, this well-organized, easy-to-use portal site should be your first stop for information about laws, services, and information related to work and employment. FirstGov for Workers pulls together information from dozens of offices and agencies. You'll find the sections on "rights and protections" and "disabilities resources" particularly useful.

Health Care Financing Administration

http://www.hcfa.gov/medicaid/hipaa/

This government agency administers the portion of the U.S. Health Insurance Portability and Accountability Act of 1996 (HIPAA) that deals with protecting health coverage for workers and their families when they change or lose their jobs. Follow the links for frequently asked questions, consumer information, and HIPAA Online, an interactive tool to help you understand your rights.

Walkers in Darkness

www.walkers.org

The Walkers Web site encompasses discussion forums, live chat, and five mailing lists about various aspects of mood disorders, as well as copious information about diagnoses, medication, therapy, and related subjects. There's even a place where members can post their photos, share Web pages, and announce their birthdays. This is a genuine online community with a big heart.

Wing of Madness

www.wingofmadness.com

One of the oldest depression sites online, Wing of Madness offers articles about depression, a regular newsletter, a bookstore with selections recommended by site owner Deborah Gray, and message boards and live chat where users can connect with each other for information and support. Don't miss Gray's thoughtful, compassionate essay about "What to Do (On and Off the Web) While You're Waiting for Your Antidepressant to Kick In."

Recommended Books on Depression

Darkness Visible: A Memoir of Madness by William Styron (Vintage, 1992)—People who have experienced depression sometimes say it's impossible to describe in a way that will make others understand how they feel. Styron captures in harrowing detail the depressive episode in 1985 that nearly drove him to suicide before he could best it. A dark and beautiful memoir in just eighty-four remarkable pages.

Feeling Good: The New Mood Therapy by David D. Burns, M.D. (Wholecare, 1999)—Written by a leader in the field of cognitive therapy, this groundbreaking best-seller shows you exactly how changing the way you think can change the way you feel. Recent studies have actually shown that just reading *Feeling Good* helps people recover more quickly from depression. But don't just read it; do the exercises. This revised edition also includes a hefty section on medication, including up-to-date information about drug interactions and side effects.

Overcoming Depression by Demitri F. Papolos, M.D., and Janice Papolos (Harper Perennial, 1997)—Since its first publication in 1987, this clearly written, comprehensive look at depression as a disease has sold hundreds of thousands of copies and is now in its third edition. Doctors often recommend it to their patients. If you have questions about your diagnosis or treatment, this is the first place to turn.

Undoing Depression: What Therapy Doesn't Teach You and Medication Can't Give You by Richard O'Connor, Ph.D. (Little, Brown & Co., 1997)—Once professional treatment has lifted you out of the crisis stage, you're halfway to recovery. O'Connor, a therapist who has firsthand experience with depression, addresses the other half: first identifying how depression has colored your ways of thinking, acting, and relating to other people, then helping you break those patterns and replace them with more healthy habits.

Particularly Helpful Books on Career Issues

Career Anchors: Discovering Your Real Values by Edgar H. Schein (University Associates Inc., 1990)— Written in workbook form by a renowned management consultant, this book incorporates a probing series of questions that will help you determine what's important to you, how you feel about work, how you see yourself, and how to bring your priorities and values into your work life.

Creating Your Future: Personal Strategic Planning for Professionals by George L. Morrisey (Berrett-Koehler, 1992)—Full of worksheets and checklists, this book helps you plot your career path using the same concepts large businesses apply to steer their overall strategy. Although Morrisey is clearly writing for white-collar professionals and consultants toiling in the corporate vineyard, his recommendations are useful to anyone, from artist to mechanic.

Do What You Are by Paul D. Tieger and Barbara Barron-Tieger (Little, Brown & Co., 2001)—For ten years, this has been the most popular book on using the Myers-Briggs Type Inventory (MBTI) to explore your strengths and uncover the ideal career for your personality type. Now in its third edition, it's been updated to include information about new career fields and resources available on the Internet.

We Are All Self-Employed: The New Social Contract for Working in a Changed World by Cliff Hakim (Berrett-Koehler, 1994)—A forceful, encouraging exploration of the new reality of work: Even if you have what you consider a stable job, the only person responsible for your career is you. A must-read no matter what you do for a living.

▪ Index ▪

A
absenteeism, cost of, x
accommodations
  common, 53–55
  confidentiality of, 98–99
  costs of, 93–94
  defined, 50–51
  and disclosure, 67, 79
  and job interviews, 82–83, 93
  perceptions of, 61–62
  proving, 60–61, 103–4
  reasonable, 50, 73, 85, 93–94,
    96, 97
  requesting, 51–53, 62–63,
    72–74, 79–81
  See also disclosure;
    discrimination
ADA. *See* Americans with
  Disabilities Act (ADA)
alcohol, as depressant, 24
Alcoholics Anonymous (AA), 10
American Psychological
  Association (APA), 131–32
Americans with Disabilities Act
  (ADA), 43–63
  assistance centers, 55, 127–30
  claiming your rights, xi,
    43–44, 49–50, 71–72, 74,
    103–4
  and depression, 46–49, 50
  described, 43–44
  disclosure requirements, 67,
    75–76, 79
  employer responsibilities,
    84–85, 88, 98

enforcement guidances, 46
government employees, 56–57
importance of, 45–46
medical leave provisions,
  95–96
resources, 130–31
sections of, 44–45, 101–2
and treatment, 57–59
Web site information, 127–31
See also accommodations;
  disclosure; discrimination
aminoketone, 7
Anafranil, 7
antidepressants
  and chemical dependency
    recovery, 10–11
  and discrimination, 59–60
  physiology of, 5
  required by employer, 94–95
anxiousness, feelings of, 17
APA. See American
  Psychological Association
  (APA)
apathy, 17–18
atypical depression, 3
avoidance, 18–19

B
baby blues. *See* postpartum
  depression
Barron-Tieger, Barbara, 139
Bazelon Center. *See* Judge
  David L. Bazelon Center for
  Mental Health Law

About the Authors

Fawn Fitter has written about careers and workplace issues, as well as many other topics, for dozens of publications ranging from *Computerworld* to *Cosmopolitan*. After a bout of major depression left her unable to work for several months, she discovered that many people were, like her, struggling with concerns about how to integrate the illness into their working lives. That experience inspired her to write *Working in the Dark*.

Fawn is an active member of the American Society of Journalists and Authors and the National Writers Union. She lives and works in San Francisco.

Beth Gulas has frequently worked with employees in crisis as a specialist in corporate critical intervention. Many of the anecdotes in *Working in the Dark* are drawn directly from her practice as president of WorkForce Management, a consulting firm specializing in helping companies anticipate, evaluate, and manage change. Her client list includes well-known companies such as Fidelity Investments, Polaroid, GTE, and Merrill Lynch as well as small entrepreneurial ventures.

In addition to her twenty years of experience in business, management, and organizational development, Beth is a licensed mental health counselor. She divides her time between Wellesley, Massachusetts, and Los Angeles.

Hazelden Publishing and Educational Services is a division of the Hazelden Foundation, a not-for-profit organization. Since 1949, Hazelden has been a leader in promoting the dignity and treatment of people afflicted with the disease of chemical dependency.

The mission of the foundation is to improve the quality of life for individuals, families, and communities by providing a national continuum of information, education, and recovery services that are widely accessible; to advance the field through research and training; and to improve our quality and effectiveness through continuous improvement and innovation.

Stemming from that, the mission of this division is to provide quality information and support to people wherever they may be in their personal journey—from education and early intervention, through treatment and recovery, to personal and spiritual growth.

Although our treatment programs do not necessarily use everything Hazelden publishes, our bibliotherapeutic materials support our mission and the Twelve Step philosophy upon which it is based. We encourage your comments and feedback.

The headquarters of the Hazelden Foundation are in Center City, Minnesota. Additional treatment facilities are located in Chicago, Illinois; New York, New York; Plymouth, Minnesota; St. Paul, Minnesota; and West Palm Beach, Florida. At these sites, we provide a continuum of care for men and women of all ages. Our Plymouth facility is designed specifically for youth and families.

For more information on Hazelden, please call **1-800-257-7800.** Or you may access our World Wide Web site on the Internet at **www.hazelden.org.**